A Concise Dictionary of Correct English

compiled by
B. A. Phythian

HODDER AND STOUGHTON
LONDON SYDNEY AUCKLAND TORONTO

British Library Cataloguing in Publication Data
Phythian, Brian Arthur

A concise dictionary of correct English
1. English language – Dictionaries
I. Title
423   PE1625

ISBN 0-340-24059-8
ISBN 0-340-24060-1 Pbk

First published 1979

Printed and bound in Great Britain for
Hodder and Stoughton Educational,
a division of Hodder and Stoughton Ltd,
Mill Road, Dunton Green, Sevenoaks, Kent,
by Butler & Tanner Ltd, Frome and London

Preface

This book is intended for those who would like to brush up their English grammar and be guided round some of the more common pitfalls in the use of English. It is hoped that those who find the book useful may be led on to a study of those much greater works to which all students of English usage are indebted, and from which I have often and gratefully drawn: Eric Partridge's *Usage and Abusage*, Fowler's *Modern English Usage*, and Gowers' *Complete Plain Words* (revised by Fraser) which, though initially commissioned to improve Civil Service English, remains perhaps the best guide to correct English for the general reader. I gladly record also my debt to *The Concise Oxford Dictionary*, from which I have taken most of the definitions I have quoted.

Many of the entries in the following pages require the reader to have a working knowledge of the principal parts of speech. Victims of the regrettable failure of English schools, during the past fifteen years or so, to supply this knowledge are invited to begin their perusal of this book by studying the entries under verb, noun, adverb, adjective, pronoun, preposition and conjunction, together with those under sentence and clause.

If any entry contains a word in bold print, that word has an entry to itself at the appropriate place alphabetically.

The following abbreviations are used:

C.O.D.	*The Concise Oxford Dictionary* (The Clarendon Press, Oxford)
Gowers	*The Complete Plain Words*, by Sir Ernest Gowers, revised by Sir Bruce Fraser (H.M.S.O.)
Fowler	*A Dictionary of Modern English Usage*, by H. W. Fowler (The Clarendon Press, Oxford)
Partridge	*Usage and Abusage*, by Eric Partridge (Hamish Hamilton Ltd)

I am grateful to my wife for checking the typescript, to Mrs Stella Lister for typing it, and to all the journalists, broadcasters and writers (notably the authors of the stunningly illiterate *Cambridge Students' Prospectus, 1978*) who have supplied the examples of English I have cited. None has been invented.

Keston, Kent   B. A. P.
1979

A

a and **an** are called the indefinite articles in English. In general, *a* is used before words beginning with a **consonant** (*a pole*) and *an* before a **vowel** (*an aperture*). There are a few exceptions: the consonant *h* is sometimes silent (as in *honest, hour*, etc.); *an* is used before words beginning with a silent *h* (*an honourable action*) but not before a sounded *h* (*a house*). The vowel *u* and the vowel-sound *eu* are sometimes pronounced like a consonant, with a *y* sound (as in *union* and *European*, etc.); *a* is used before words with this initial sound (*a useless article*), but not otherwise (*an unusual event*).

See **definite article, hotel**.

abbreviation. The normal rule is to put full stops after abbreviations, e.g. *a.m.* Full stops are not necessary after *Mr, Mrs* and *Dr*, nor with abbreviations that have become words in their own right (e.g. *phone, fridge, pub*, etc.). It is becoming increasingly common to omit full stops from abbreviations, especially when an abbreviation is used more frequently than the full version and is beginning to assume the status of a word: TUC, BBC, MP, RAF, VAT, USA. If in doubt, use full stops.

Note the punctuation of the abbreviations *don't, isn't, I'm, he's, they're*, etc., where the apostrophe indicates an omitted letter. See **apostrophe 2**.

If an abbreviation concludes a sentence, it is common (but not obligatory) to put two full stops, one to punctuate the abbreviation, the second to indicate the end of the sentence. Two stops, however, are never found in print.

See **it's, St**.

abdicate. See **arrogate**.

abdomen may be pronounced with the stress on the second syllable (to rhyme with *toe*), or on the first.

abrogate. See **arrogate**.

absolute construction. See **verb 5(b)**.

abstract noun. See **noun**.

academic means *scholarly*. It has also come to mean *unimportant*, or *of interest to very few*, as in

The result of today's match is academic, because

1

Manchester United already have enough points to assure them of the championship.

The development of the word has been *academic = scholarly = unpractical = irrelevant*. This last meaning of *academic* is worth resisting, if only because it is confusing that a word should be both a compliment (*scholarly*) and a term of mild abuse (*irrelevant*).

accent. When a word with more than one **syllable** is pronounced, one of the syllables is emphasised more strongly than the others, e.g. the first syllable in *flippant*, the second in *monotony*, the third in *interfere*. This stress is known as *accent*.

Words which are written identically may be pronounced differently: *object* as a noun has the accent on the first syllable; as a verb it has the accent on the second.

accessary means *helper in* or *one privy to* an act, usually criminal. *Accessory* is found usually as a noun meaning *small object* or *part* contributing or subordinate to a greater whole, as in *car accessories* (e.g. seat-covers), *costume accessories* (e.g. jewellery). The two spellings should not be confused.

accommodate is one of the most frequently mis-spelt words in English. Double c, double m.

accompanied by is correct when referring to persons:

He was accompanied by his daughter.

Of things, *accompanied with* is correct.

He accompanied his speech with blows on the table.

accusative. A noun or pronoun is said to be *in the accusative* when it is the object of a verb or preposition. See **preposition 2, pronoun, verb 4.** Since only pronouns have different forms in the accusative and the **nominative** in English, the word *accusative* has little importance except with regard to pronouns.

acetic pertains to vinegar, and the *ce* is pronounced *see*. *Ascetic* = austere, severely abstinent; *an ascetic* is a person who practises severe self-discipline, often retiring into solitude for this purpose. The *scet* is pronounced *set*.

activate means *make active*. It is best reserved to define physical or chemical action. *Actuate* has the advantage of meaning both *move to action* and *serve as motive to*, as in

It appears to have been malice that actuated him.

active and passive. A verb is said to be in the active voice when its **subject** is performing the action of the verb:

> The mob *broke* the windows.

When the subject is being acted on, the verb is said to be passive:

> The windows *were broken* by the mob.

It is sometimes said that use of the active and avoidance of the passive help to create a good strong style.

The infinitive has active and passive forms, in both the present (*to strike, to be struck*) and the past tense (*to have struck, to have been struck*). For an explanation of *infinitive* see **verb 5 (a)**.

actual and actually. It is worth noting how often these words are used unnecessarily, especially the former in the common phrase **in actual fact**. All facts are actual, and there is therefore no need to refer to any particular one as being *actual*. The word *actually* is usually used to give the speaker a moment in which to think.

actuate. See **activate**.

acumen (= keen discernment) should be pronounced with the emphasis on the second syllable, which is as in *queue*.

acute. See **chronic**.

adapt and **adopt**. The former means *alter, make suitable for a purpose*. The latter means *accept, take (an idea, etc.) from someone else*. One may make an extra bedroom by *adopting* one's neighbour's plan and *adapting* the garage.

adaptor, an electrical fitment, not to be confused with *adapter*, a person who adapts books (e.g. turns them into plays).

adequate. See **tautology**.

adjectival clause. See **clause 2**.

adjective. A word that describes a noun (an *attractive* possibility; *seventy-six* trombones).

    1. When an adjective is used in comparing two things, its form may change:

> This route is *quick*.
>
> *but* This route is *quicker* than that one.

Quicker is called the *comparative* or *comparative degree* of the adjective *quick*. The comparative may be formed by adding *-er* to the adjective, but adjectives of more than one syllable usually form the comparative by using the word *more*, to avoid ugliness of sound:

3

Lunch was *expensive*.

but Lunch was *more expensive* than I expected.

2. When an adjective is used in comparing more than two persons or things, the *superlative* or *superlative degree* is used, either by adding *-est* to the adjective or by using *most*:

That is the *strangest* story I have ever heard.

He is the *most experienced* player in the team.

3. A few adjectives form the comparative and superlative irregularly:

bad	worse	worst
good	better	best
much ⎫ many ⎭	more	most
little	less	least

4. It is a common fault of grammar to use the comparative degree instead of the superlative when more than two items are being compared:

Which do you like *most* (not *more*) – wine, women or song?

It is also wrong to use the superlative instead of the comparative when only two items are being compared:

Which is the *better* (not *best*) bargain – this or that?

The rules should be strictly observed. Use the comparative form (fast, *faster*, fastest; spacious, *more spacious*, most spacious) when comparing two people or things, and use the superlative form (big, bigger, *biggest*; extravagant, more extravagant, *most extravagant*) when comparing more than two:

the *taller* of the two; the *largest* of the four; the *more attractive* of the two; the *most attractive* of the four.

5. When used as adjectives, *this* and *that* have plural forms, *these* and *those*. In accordance with the normal rules of agreement the singular form should be used with a singular noun, and the plural form with a plural noun:

those kind of people should be *that kind* (or *those kinds*)

these sort of shops should be *this sort* (or *these sorts*)

Avoid similarly *those class*, *these type*, etc.

6. Care should be taken when placing the adjective. Note the difference between *women's second-hand clothing* and *second-hand women's clothing*.

See also **pronoun 5**.

adopt. See **adapt**.

4

adverb. A word that describes a verb, an adjective or another adverb:

> The band played *loudly* and *inaccurately* (describing the verb *played*).
>
> On occasions the noise was *unbearably* loud (describing the adjective *loud*).
>
> We left *very* early (describing the adverb *early*).

1. An adverb normally indicates how, when, where or in what degree the action of a verb takes place:

> Think *carefully*.   Come *tomorrow*.
>
> Look *up*.   It was *partially* destroyed.

An adverb describing an adjective or another adverb normally describes degree, extent or intensity:

> You ate *too* much. They were *exceptionally* kind.
>
> That's *quite* a good idea.

An adverb which describes a verb describes the *action* of that verb. Some verbs which do not denote action are followed by adjectives, not adverbs:

> She *is* tall. He *looks* ill. The results *are* good.
>
> It *appears* strange. It *seems* wrong. It *feels* smooth.

2. Some adverbs, like adjectives, change their form when comparisons are being used.

(*a*)   How *long* will the journey last?

> It will take *longer* than you expect.

Longer is the *comparative degree* of the adverb *long*. The comparative is used when two items are being compared. Most adverbs form the comparative by using *more*:

> Time passes *more quickly* when one is occupied (i.e. more quickly than it does when one is idle).

(*b*)   The car goes fast, the train goes faster, but the aeroplane goes *fastest* of all.

Fastest is the *superlative degree* of the adverb *fast* (of which *faster* is the comparative). The superlative is used when more than two things are being compared, as in the example quoted. Most adverbs form the superlative by using *most*:

> Of all the performers, she danced *most* gracefully.

(*c*) Some adverbs form the comparative and superlative irregularly:

badly	worse	worst
little	less	least
well	better	best

3. It is important to place the adverb as close as possible to the word it describes. Whoever penned the sentence

The Chief Constable ordered the rioters to be arrested
indignantly

may have intended to report that the Chief Constable ordered
his men to experience indignation while arresting the rioters; it
is more likely that it was the Chief Constable who experienced
indignation, so the adverb *indignantly* should have been placed
adjacent to *ordered* (i.e. before it), not adjacent to *arrested*. For a
more subtle illustration of the same point, see **only**.

4. The word *real* is an adjective. Its adverbial form is *really*.

The team played real well.

They've had a real good time.

are incorrect, because the adverbial *really* is required to describe
the adverb *well* and the adjective *good*.

adverbial clause. See **clause 2**.

adversary is pronounced with the stress on the first syllable.

adverse. See **averse**.

advice, advise. One can understand confusion between **practice**
and **practise** which are pronounced alike, but there is less excuse
for confusion between *advice* (noun) and *advise* (verb) since their
spelling is in accordance with familiar rules of pronunciation, i.e.
the final syllable of the noun is pronounced *ice*, and the final syllable of the verb is pronounced *ize*.

advisedly does not mean *having taken advice*, but *carefully, after consideration*.

affect is often confused with *effect*. The words have a number of
meanings, but those which are most often confused are the verbs:

affect: have an effect on.

effect: bring about, accomplish.

It is perhaps helpful to remember that *affect* is always a verb
(except in the specialised language of psychology) but that *effect*
can be both noun and verb:

Smoking may have an effect on your health. (noun)

To give up smoking may effect an improvement in your
health. (verb)

Smoking may affect your health.

Affect is sometimes used loosely. The sports journalist who wrote,
of a player in a tennis match,

In the third set, he was much affected by the crowd.

failed to say how the player was affected: was he hindered, distracted,

angered, or helped in some way? Avoid *affect* if a more precise word
is available.

afflict. See **inflict**.

after. See **behind, following**.

again is unnecessary in *renew again*, *repeat again*, *recur again*, *revive again*
and with any other verb which contains the notion of *again* within
itself (consult the dictionary under *re-*) and which therefore needs no
assistance from the superfluous adverb *again*. See **tautology**.

aggravate means *increase the gravity of* a condition already serious or,
often, unpleasant: *His accident aggravated his limp*. Opinions on the very
common use of the word to mean *annoy* or *irritate* vary from 'colloquial' (*C.O.D.*) to 'uneducated' (Fowler); it is probably best to avoid
this usage, despite its antiquity (1611), if only because uncontroversial
synonyms are readily available.

aggravation, in the sense of *bother, trouble, irritation*, is slangy and
should be avoided because it derives from a definition of **aggravate**
that is still regarded as dubious. Use *aggravation* to mean *worsening*.

ago must not be confused with *previously*. *Ago*=past, gone by (*ten years
ago*), since (*long ago*). *Previously*=before. Note the differences in *I saw
'Hamlet' a year ago; I had last seen it three years previously* (i.e. three
years *before* the performance a year ago).

ago that, not *ago since*, when *ago* is followed by a clause describing the
event which is being dated:
> It is twenty-five years *ago that* they emigrated.
> or It is twenty-five years *since* they emigrated.
but not
> It is twenty-five years *ago since* they emigrated.
because *ago* and *since* have the same meaning, and *ago* requires *that*.

agreement. As a simple general rule, words or groups of words that
go together should be placed close together.
> For sale: chair suitable for lady with wide seat.
This makes sense, but it is courteous to assume that the advertiser intended to suggest that the wide seat belonged to *chair*, not *lady*. The
phrase *with wide seat* should have been placed after *chair*.
> As a boy, his mother had neglected him.
is a less immediately obvious example of the same error. *As a boy*
leads the reader to expect that the sentence will continue to say something about him: instead the direction of the grammar changes, and

7

his mother is introduced in a way which implies that she had had an irregular childhood. The sentence should be corrected by placing *as a boy* after *him*, which it describes. Alternatively,

> *As a boy, he* had been neglected by his mother.

Other examples: from a recent newspaper

> The explosives were found by *a security man in a plastic bag*.

The phrase *in a plastic bag* belongs to *found* and should be placed after it. From a mother's letter to school:

> Being cold, I kept Ian at home today.

The grammar implies that *I* was *being cold*; this is not the intended meaning.

See **everybody, like 5, only, or, sort.**

akin to, not *akin with*.

alibi has a specific meaning: an alibi is a plea that, at a certain time, one was elsewhere. There is no good reason for using it as a showy and inaccurate substitute for the perfectly adequate word *excuse*.

all kind of is incorrect. While *all* is singular when it means *the whole amount, quantity or extent of* (e.g. *all day*), it is plural when it means *the entire number of* (e.g. *all the women*). It is this plural sense which is intended in *all kind of* and so the noun *kind* must be made plural (*all kinds of*). Alternatively, avoid *all* and use a singular adjective (*every kind of*). *All manner of*, however, is correct.

all right. This is the correct spelling. *Alright* is always wrong.

all together consists of an adjective and an adverb:

> The guests arrived all together.

means

> All (*adjective*) the guests arrived together (*adverb*).

Altogether is quite different – an adverb meaning *on the whole* or *totally*:

> He spent five pounds altogether.

The two spellings should not be confused.

allegory. Description of a subject (usually abstract) under the guise of some other subject (usually in terms of people, places or events). *Animal Farm* deals with certain aspects of communism by means of a story about animals; *Pilgrim's Progress* describes the author's spiritual life in the form of a tale about a hazardous journey. *Allegory* may also be found in painting.

allergic has a precise and useful medical sense, an *allergy* being an adverse physical reaction to particular physical substances such as foods, pollens, etc. It may be legitimately jocular to claim to be *allergic to* a certain politician, but the over-use of *allergic to* to express mere dislike is to be avoided, on the grounds that a precise and useful expression should not be weakened by being over-used in a general sense for which another and adequate expression (e.g. *hostile to, averse to*) already exists.

alliteration is the use of the same initial letter (usually a **consonant**) or syllable in successive words. Frequently used in advertisements to add emphasis (*Philosan fortifies the over-forties*), it has its main literary importance in poetry, less frequently in prose, to add point, beauty of sound, variety or humour.

allusion is, properly, indirect or implied reference. Likewise *allude* means *refer indirectly*. This useful shade of meaning is destroyed if *allusion* is used, as it often is, when *reference* or *mention* would be correct, or if *allude to* is used instead of simply *mean* or *refer to*. Keep *allusion* and *allude* to signify indirectness of reference.

almost needs careful placing:
>We almost sold the house (i.e. but we didn't).
>We sold almost all our furniture (i.e. but we kept some).

alright. See **all right**.

also is not a conjunction, and so the following is wrong:
>Please let us know your new address, also your
>telephone number.

This kind of use of *also* is common in speech, but in writing the conjunction *and* should be inserted before *also*, or instead of it. Not being a conjunction, *also* cannot be used to tack words on to a sentence in this way.

alternate should be used when referring to two things, persons, etc. As an adjective (with the accent on the second syllable: as a verb it has the accent on the first) it means *coming each after one of the other kind*:
>The milkman calls on alternate days.

means that a day on which he calls is followed by one on which he does not, after which the same two-day pattern is repeated.
>He also delivers eggs on Tuesdays or alternately on
>Thursdays.

alternative

means that he will deliver them on a Tuesday or on *every other* Thursday. What the writer of this sentence probably meant to say is that one can choose to have eggs delivered on a Tuesday or a Thursday. He probably intended to say *alternatively* which (unlike *alternately*) always implies a choice. In fact, neither adverb is necessary:

He also delivers eggs on Tuesdays or Thursdays.

See **alternative**.

alternative, as a noun, denotes either of two possible courses. Strictly speaking, there are never several alternatives, only two; it is ungrammatical to speak of *the only (other) alternative* because, by definition, an alternative is always the 'only (other)' course of action available if one alternative has been rejected, and so *only (other)* is unnecessary. If more than two courses of action are available, one has *choices* but not *alternatives*.

Many would say that the above definition is too strict, and that usage now allows *alternative* when there are more than two choices.

The idea of choice is implicit in *alternative*. As an adjective, it is often used as a substitute for *other, new, revised*, etc.; this is incorrect.

When applying for tickets, please give an alternative date.

is correct, because applicants are being invited to exercise choice.

Friday's performance is cancelled, and ticket-holders will be informed when alternative arrangements have been made.

is not correct, because no choice is being offered: *revised* or *other* should have been used instead of *alternative*.

alternatively is often used superfluously, as in *Come tomorrow or alternatively the day after*, where *alternatively* adds nothing not already expressed by *or*.

altogether. See **all together**.

ambiguity. *Bearded company director Patrick Phillips claimed he watched his wife committing adultery through a spy-hole he had drilled in his bedroom ceiling* (from a newspaper article).

One could quote countless examples of unclear or ludicrous statements resulting from slipshod grammar (see **agreement, as well as, comma**). In the example quoted, *through* belongs to *watched* and should therefore be placed nearer to it, instead of next to *committing adultery* (... *claimed his wife committed adultery while he watched her through a spy-hole* ...).

Newspapers seem particularly prone to unintentional ambiguities, as in the headline

Sun-suit Schoolgirl is Suspended by Head.

ambivalent means *having conflicting or irreconcilable feelings about something or somebody*, and should not be loosely used to mean *undecided*, *indecisive* or *ambiguous*. Like many new words imported into general use from the language of psychology, *ambivalent* has its uses, though it is currently overworked, and often used inaccurately. There are few occasions when *feel ambivalent towards* is preferable to *have mixed feelings about*.

amiable and **amicable** both mean *friendly*, but the former is applied to people and their natures (*an amiable disposition*), the latter to the means by which friendship may be displayed (*an amicable arrangement*, *relationship*, etc.).

amid and **amidst**. Both are correct, but the latter is slightly old-fashioned and literary.

among and **amongst**. Both are correct, but the latter is less common than it used to be. *Among* is always followed by a plural (*among his belongings*), or by a singular noun with a plural sense (e.g. *among their number; among the crowd*). The common expressions *among other things* and *among others* are often used when *along with/besides/in addition to/other things* would be more precise.

See **between** for an important distinction between *among* and *between*.

amoral. See **immoral**.

amount of applies to volume (*a large amount of work*); *number of* applies to separable items (*a large number of jobs*).

and. The old rule that one should not begin a sentence with *And* is worth observing, though it is not so much a rule as a piece of advice. There are occasions when special emphasis may be added by ignoring the advice.

If *and* links two singular nouns, they form a plural and need a plural verb. The following (from the *Cambridge Students' Prospectus, 1978*) is wrong:

The quality and the price of food *has* become more reasonable.

For wrong uses of *and* with certain pronouns, see **and which** and **but who**. See also **comma 8** and **conjunction**.

and additionally is an unnecessary expression. Use one word or the other, but not both.

and/or should be avoided, even at the expense of having to use a longer sentence. It may be useful bureaucratic shorthand, but that does not excuse its ugliness.

and which may only be used to link what follows with a previous clause beginning with *which*:

> The garden, which had been so carefully tended, and which was now at its best, adjoined the river.

is correct: the conjunction *and* links the two clauses beginning with *which*.

> The garden, so carefully tended and which was now at its best ...

is wrong, because *and* is linking a phrase (*so carefully tended*) and a clause (*which was now* ...), and conjunctions can link only those grammatical units which are of equal status (two phrases, two clauses, etc.). See **conjunction**.

The same applies to clauses beginning *and who, and whose, and where*, etc., and equally to *but which, but who*, etc.

angry should be followed by *with* when one is *angry with* a person, and by *at* when one is *angry at* anything.

antagonist. See **protagonist**.

anti-social means *opposed to the principles on which society is based*. It is correct to describe as anti-social any behaviour which disturbs the equilibrium of society, offends right-thinking members of society or is, in a word, un-neighbourly, but it is a cheapening of a useful word to use *anti-social* as a substitute for *unsociable* or even *grumpy*.

anticipate does not mean *expect*, despite general opinion. It means *forestall* (a person or thing); *consider, discuss or realise beforehand*; *look forward to*. The word is used correctly in

> Before you begin, try to anticipate the difficulties.

> Such a disaster could not have been anticipated.

Gowers offers useful advice: do not use *anticipate* before *that* or *to* followed by a verb, as in

> I anticipate that he will arrive late.

It is possible that usage will ultimately decree that *anticipate* means *expect*, but for the moment the correct meaning is worth insisting on.

antonym. A word of contrary meaning to another. *Weak* is the antonym of *strong*. The opposite of *antonym* is **synonym**.

anxiety, **anxious** should be followed by *about*, not *of*.

any place, as in *I can't find it any place*, is American, and is an unnecessary substitute for the English *anywhere*.

anybody and **anyone** are singular. Care should be taken to ensure that any verb of which one of them is the subject, or any pronoun relating to one of them, is likewise singular:

Anyone *is* welcome to join provided that *he* pays *his* subscription (NOT *they* pay *their* subscription).

In such a sentence, *he* does duty for *he or she*.
See **everybody.**

anytime does not exist. It must be spelt as two words, *any time*.

apostrophe. A raised comma (') used to indicate
1. possession:
the town's bus service; workers' wages.
For a full explanation, see **possessive.**
2. the omission of letters in contractions:
I'll (I will); I'm (I am); I've (I have); he's (he has or he is); won't (will not); don't (do not); can't (cannot); shan't (shall not); let's (let us); isn't (is not); we're (we are); hadn't (had not), etc.
Such contractions are frequent in speech. In writing they should be reserved for informal occasions.

In some contexts (e.g. in a story which contains the actual words spoken by a character), apostrophes are often used to denote letters omitted in the course of slangy, casual or dialect speech:
'cos (because); bloomin'; a pint o' beer; what's 'e doin'?

appear is sometimes wrongly used, as in
I don't appear to be able to find it.
which should be
I appear to be unable (*or* not to be able) to find it.
It is the ability, not the appearing, which is lacking.

appendix has the plural form *appendices*. *Appendixes* is permitted, but is unusual.

applicable is pronounced with stress on the first syllable, not the second.

appraise means *estimate, form a judgment about*, and should not be confused with *apprise* (=inform). A jury, in the course of *appraising* evidence, may wish to *appraise* themselves of a point of law by return-ing to court to ask a judge for guidance.

appreciate means *esteem highly*, *be sensitive to*, *set a value on* (as well as *raise/rise in value*) and the word should not be devalued by being used when a word with less feeling (such as *understand*, *realise*) would be more appropriate.

approximate(ly) means *very near(ly)*, and it is wrong to use *very approximate(ly)* when what is meant is *very rough(ly)*, i.e. not *approxi-mate(ly)* at all.

apt to. See **liable to**.

arguably is a fashionable and unnecessary substitute for *perhaps*. If it must be used, it means *it may be argued (that)* and should be confined to circumstances that are worth arguing about.

argument is frequently mis-spelt. The *e* of *argue* is dropped as in *argu-able*, *arguing*, *argumentative*, etc.

arrogate: claim unduly. Not to be confused with *abdicate* (= renounce) or *abrogate* (= cancel, repeal). One *abrogates* a treaty, *abdicates* responsi-bility, and *arrogates* to oneself the right to do something.

as 1. The two sentences
>I am not as fat as *I was*.
>He is not as fat as *I am*.

are obviously correct, yet a shortened version of the second sentence
>He is not as fat as *I*.

would be regarded as rather pretentious. The usual version would be
>He is not as fat as *me*.

though the change from the correct nominative *I* (subject of the omitted verb *am*) to the incorrect accusative *me* is both unnecessary and indefensible.

This is probably a case where popular usage will eventually super-sede correct grammar, which states that *as* cannot be used as a pre-position, only as
(*a*) an adverb: I came *as* quickly as I could.
(*b*) a conjunction: I came as quickly *as* I could.
(*c*) a relative pronoun: In such countries *as* France, motorways are toll-roads.

2. Some sentences beginning with *as* trap the writer into illiteracy. A letter (from a university teacher) to a national newspaper begins:

As a Professor of Sociology, one would expect John
Barron Mays to have produced at least one fact to back
up his statement.

After the italicised adjectival phrase, the reader instinctively
expects that the noun or pronoun it describes will follow immediately. The above sentence therefore means that *one* (i.e. the writer)
is a Professor of Sociology. Only later does it become clear that
the writer is not, but that J. B. Mays is. The letter should have read
either

As a Professor of Sociology, John Barron Mays should
have ...

or

One would have expected John Barron Mays, as a
Professor of Sociology, to produce ...

so that the adjectival phrase *as a Professor of Sociology* is unambiguously related to the correct noun, *J. B. Mays*.
See **agreement**.

as ... as. There is sometimes a temptation to drop the second *as* in comparisons:

The town is as big if not bigger than Hastings.

Two constructions (*as big as Hastings* and *bigger than Hastings*) are run
together; the omission of the second *as* of *as big as* produces a sentence
which, grammatically, means

The town is as big than, if not bigger than, Hastings.

which is not good English. Comparisons using *as ... as* must have
a second *as*:

The town is as big as if not bigger than Hastings.

See **as well as, equally**.

as and when says nothing more than *as* or *when* alone can.

as follows is always correct, even when what follows is plural.

as how is incorrect for *how*, *that*, or *whether* in such uses as

I don't see *as how* I could be expected to know that.

as to should be used with care. Before *when, who, what, how, whether,*
etc., it is often superfluous, as in

He has asked to be informed as to how/why the
error occurred.

This should read

He has asked to be informed how (*or* why) the error occurred.

as to whether

There are circumstances when *as to* has a legitimate function; when it has none, omit it.

as to whether signifies nothing that *whether* cannot signify on its own.

as well as should be used with care. *The audience sang as well as the choir* is ambiguous; did the audience sing *in addition to* the choir, or *as excellently as* the choir? If the former, insert a comma after *sang*; if the latter, insert *did* after *choir*.

Note also

Their job is to pack biscuits as well as making them.

Because *as well as* is here a conjunction meaning *and not only*, there is no good reason for switching from the infinitive *to pack* to the participle *making*: it would be better English to say

Their job is to pack biscuits as well as (to) make them.

so that the conjunction links two similar grammatical units, as it should. However, the idiom *as well as*+participle is now very common. See **conjunction**.

as yet. The *as* is quite unnecessary and should be omitted.

ascetic. See **acetic**.

assemble. See **tautology**.

assonance is the deliberate repetition of a vowel-sound in a sentence or a line of poetry for musical effect or for emphasis. Unintentional assonance is clumsy; Fowler quotes:

Worser and worser grows the plight of the Globe over
the oversea trade figures.

auspicious: conducive to success; of good omen; prosperous. An *auspicious* beginning is one that promises a favourable continuation and conclusion. Signs which are *auspicious* promise good fortune. Times which are *auspicious* are prosperous ones.

The word is sometimes wrongly used as if it meant *special* or *distinguished*, especially in the phrase *this auspicious occasion*.

authoritative, not *authoritive*.

automaton may become either *automata* or *automatons* in the plural. The word is Greek and the alternative plurals are classical and English respectively.

avenge. See **revenge**.

averse to means *unwilling, disinclined, opposed to*, and is usually found in negative forms, such as

He was not averse to the idea.
meaning
He was not unwilling to entertain the idea.
It should not be confused with *adverse (to)* meaning *hostile (to)*, as in *adverse criticism*.

Averse may also be followed by *from*.

aversion is normally followed by *to*, though *from* and *for* are permitted. The following, from a recent speech by a Q.C., is wrong:
The employees have a general aversion of doing overtime.

awake and **awaken** mean the same, but their past tenses are often confused:

Verb	Past tense	Past participle
awake	awoke	awaked
awaken	awakened	awakened

In view of its relative simplicity, *awaken* is to be preferred. *Awoken* does not exist. See **wake**.

awhile is an adverb meaning *for a short time*. It is sometimes confused with *a while*. In
Let's sit down for a while.
while is a noun meaning *period of time*, as it is in
I haven't seen him for a long while.
One can say
Let's sit down awhile (i.e. for a short time).
or
Let's sit down for a while (i.e. for a time).
but not
Let's sit down for awhile.

B

back is superfluous in *repay back*, *revert back*, *return back*, *refer back* and with any other verb which contains the notion of *back* within itself, usually in the prefix *re* (see any dictionary under *re-*), and which therefore needs no further assistance in the form of the unnecessary adverb *back*. See **tautology**.

barely should be followed by *when*, not *than*:
> The strike had barely finished *when* fresh trouble broke
> out.

See also **hardly** and **scarcely**. *No sooner ... than* is, however, correct.

basic. See **basically**.

basically is much over-used and can, more often than not, be omitted without detriment to good sense. The same is true of *basic* in such expressions as *the basic cause, the basic reason*; unless there are several causes or reasons, of which the *basic* or fundamental one is being referred to, omit *basic*.

basis is often used unnecessarily and in long-winded expressions which are both cumbersome and jaded. For *on a weekly basis* and *on a temporary basis*, for instance, say simply *weekly* or *temporarily*. A recent government circular contains the sentence:
> Supplies of butter at reduced prices are available on a
> continuing basis.

The use of
> Supplies of butter at reduced prices are still available.

would have saved seven syllables, and been more direct and elegant.
Basis has the plural *bases* (pronounced base-ees).

basketful. See **handful**.

bathos. See **pathos**.

bear has the past tense *bore* and the past participle *borne*: *he bore a grudge; the truth was borne in upon them. Born* is also a past participle of *bear* but is confined to the sense *come into the world by birth*.

because. It is a common error to say *The reason ... is because* instead of *The reason ... is that*. It should be remembered that *because* means *for the reason that*.
> The reason we stopped was because it started to snow.

therefore means
> The reason we stopped was for the reason that ...

which is incorrect. Grammar requires
> The reason we stopped was *that* it started to snow.

or, of course,
> We stopped because it started to snow.

beg the question does not mean *fail to give a straight answer*. It means *assume the truth of something which in fact needs proving*. If one says that public schools ought to be abolished because they are *élitist* and have *paternalistic* headmasters, one is assuming that élitism and paternalism are bad things: such assumptions may be false, and have to be proved before a conclusion about the abolition of public schools can be logically made. Other question-begging words may include *liberation* (in the sense of *conquest*), *freedom-fighters* (who may be anarchists), *reactionaries* (people one disagrees with), *victimisation* (justified punishment), etc.

behind is not necessary after *follow* (nor is *after*). *Closely* or *at a distance* may be used after *follow*, as the sense demands, but *behind* is always superfluous.

behove is found only in the construction *it behoves* (*someone*) *to* (*do something*), and means *it is incumbent on* (*someone*) *to* (*do something*).

being. If you begin a sentence with an adjectival phrase introduced by *Being*, ensure that the phrase is immediately followed by the noun or pronoun which it describes, not by some unrelated noun or pronoun. The error, which is fully described at **verb 5 (b)**, is illustrated by the following, from the *Cambridge Students' Prospectus, 1978*:
> Being a small college, everyone can get to know who everyone else is.

benefit. Unlike *fit* (which has *fitted* and *fitting* as participles), *benefit* has *benefited* and *benefiting*, i.e. the *t* is not doubled.

beside. See **besides**.

besides means *in addition* (*to*), as in
> Do you play other games besides tennis?
> Besides, it is too cold to go out.

It should not be used as if it meant the same as *beside*, which means *near*, etc., as in *beside the sea-side*.

between 1. It used to be said that *between* could be used only when referring to two persons or things, and that *among* had to be used when referring to more than two. Thus *Let's divide the cost among the four of us* but *between the two of us*. This no longer holds good.

Between expresses the relationship of something to two or more surrounding things, severally and individually. *Among* expresses a relationship to them collectively and equally. Thus
> You can camp between (*not* among) the river, the wood and the wall.
> You'll have to search among (*not* between) all those papers to find it.

2. It has also been said that something can only be *between* at least two other things, and that it is therefore nonsensical to use *between* with a singular, as in

Draw a line *between each piece* of work.

The difficulty can be avoided by using *after*, but the rule is not taken seriously nowadays.

3. If *between* is followed by a conjunction, this must be *and*. The following is wrong:

The choice is between eating before we start the journey *or* having to stop on the way.

Between . . . and betweeen . . . is occasionally found, and is also wrong.

between you and I is a common error. All prepositions are followed by the accusative: under *him*, behind *us*, to *me*. *Between* is no exception. Thus *between you and me* is always right. See **preposition 2, pronoun**. The expression *in between* is an example of **tautology**: *between* is quite sufficient.

bias may become either *biased* or *biassed* in the past tense.

billion means one million million in Europe and one thousand million in America. Because the European definition is so seldom needed, it is being superseded in Britain and some other countries by the American one, e.g. in scientific usage and as standard usage in some newspapers.

blame means *find fault with, fix the responsibility on.*

Don't blame it on me.

is wrong for

Don't blame me for it.

Such misuse is very common.

blatant means *noisy; offensively and vulgarly clamorous*, but it is now so frequently used as if it meant the same as *flagrant* (=*glaring, notorious, scandalous*) as in *blatant disobedience, blatantly dishonest*, that it is probably a waste of time to complain of such quite unnecessary misuse.

blend. See **tautology**.

blond, blonde. One may say *a blonde woman* (*little girl, etc.*) or simply *a blonde*. In all other cases, use *blond* (as in *blond hair, blond complexion*).

blow has the past tense *blew* and past participle *blown*. *Blowed* exists only in colloquial exclamation (*I'll be blowed*) and it is illiterate to use it in any other way, such as in *He blowed hot and cold* or *The wind has blowed all day*.

blueprint is over-used, and is seldom preferable to *plan*. If the temptation to use *blueprint* (as a metaphor) is strong, at least let it be remembered that a blueprint is a final plan, not a rough or preliminary draft.

boor, pronounced as spelt, means *ill-mannered adult*, and should be differentiated from *bore*, meaning *boring person*.

born, borne. See **bear**.

both should be applied only to *two* persons, groups of persons, or things:
> Both Egypt, Israel and Libya are ...

is incorrect.
> *Both* is redundant in
> They are both alike.
> Both universities and polytechnics are equally affected.

> *Both* should not be followed by *as well as*, which has the same force and is therefore redundant. It is correct to say:
> The ruling will affect *both* tourists *and* residents.

or
> The ruling will affect tourists *as well as* residents.

but not
> The ruling will affect *both* tourists *as well as* residents.

both ... and. The words which form the two parts of expressions introduced by *both ... and ...* should be grammatically equivalent units.
> You should both *inform the Inspector of Taxes* and *your employer*.

should be
> You should inform both *the Inspector of Taxes* and *your employer*.

because in the first version the italicised words are not grammatically equivalent: the first group of italicised words is a sentence, the second is a noun. In the second version, both italicised expressions are of equal grammatical value, i.e. they are both nouns.

> Note too that in the first version the misplacing of *both* creates ambiguity: *you should both* can mean *both of you should*.

> For other examples of similar rules, see **either ... or 2**, **like 5**, **not only ... but (also)**.

bottleneck is an occasionally useful metaphor to describe the constriction of flow, as in
> Traffic from the motorway is invariably delayed at the

bottleneck formed by the narrow road leading into the town.

Those who use *bottleneck* should remember the origin of the expression and not speak of a *large bottleneck* or of *solving the bottleneck*.

brackets enclose a word or group of words introduced either parenthetically into a sentence, or by way of explanation. It is essential that, if a sentence contains a word or words in brackets, the sentence must make complete grammatical sense if the bracketed words are removed, i.e. the brackets and the words they enclose are additions to the sentence, not an integral and grammatical part of it.

Brackets should be used sparingly (it is easy to fall into the bad habit of using them extensively) because they can appear to be an acknowledgment by the writer that something is being inserted as an afterthought and that he has been too lazy to think out in advance what he wishes to say. Used with discretion, however, brackets can add a different tone of voice (a sort of confidential aside) to a piece of writing:

The audience applauded loudly, and the chairman (who had been asleep during most of the speech) beamed with approval.

Used too much, brackets can slow down a piece of writing or confuse the sense, causing irritation to the reader.

If what is to be put in brackets is a complete sentence, it is usually preferable to express it as a separate, new sentence, and not to put it in brackets inside another sentence.

A pair of dashes may be used as the equivalent of brackets.

Brackets are sometimes called *parentheses*.

break has the past participle *broken*, except in the slang use meaning *without money* (*I'm broke*, etc.). In all other cases use *broken*.

bucketful. See **handful**.

bulk. The expression *the bulk of* should be used only when referring to mass or volume, not when referring to number. Thus *most readers*, not *the bulk of readers*.

bureau adds *x* to form the plural.

burst, as a verb, has the past tense and past participle *burst*, never *bursted*. See **bust**.

bust, as a verb, is best regarded as slang: the most common meanings are *bankrupt* (*The business went bust*) and *broken* (*The gramophone's* *busted*). The *Shorter Oxford English Dictionary* describes *bust* as a dialect or vulgar form of *burst*, though the word has a more formal status in America.

The verb *burst* has the past tense and past participle *burst*. *Bursted* does not exist, and *busted*, being slang, is inappropriate for a formal report quoted in a recent newspaper article:

> The bags of food were busted open, and their contents
> lay on the deck.

The word required was *burst*.

but 1. As a conjunction, *but* does not mean *and*, and the following is therefore incorrect:

> For his considerable efforts, Mr Meadows now receives
> half a gallon of Cutty Sark Whisky but also the *Oxford
> English Dictionary*.

2. As a preposition, *but* followed by a pronoun requires the pronoun to be in the accusative:

> Nobody can do it but *me*.

See **between you and I**; **preposition 2**.

Occasionally, *but* + pronoun can form part of the subject of a sentence, and it would be regarded as correct to say

> Nobody but I can do it.

3. There is a superstition that it is wrong to begin a sentence with *But* and that one must use *however* instead. It is not wrong, though any over-use of sentences beginning *But* could produce monotony.

See also **help but**.

but also. See **not only ... but (also)**.

but ... however. In such sentences as

> The landlord is a surly man but the bar-maids, however,
> are always cheerful.

the words *but* and *however* are doing the same job – indicating a contrast or a change of direction in the sense. One of them is therefore redundant. Either omit *however* or replace *but* by a semi-colon.

but which. See **but who**.

but who is often used incorrectly, as in

> He was a doctor with many good qualities but who was
> unpopular.

The conjunction *but* should join grammatical units of the same kind. In the sentence quoted, *but* joins a phrase (*with many good qualities*) and a clause (*who was unpopular*). These are not equivalent grammatical units. To correct, either change the phrase to a clause

> . . . who had many good qualities but who was unpopular.

or change the clause from a subordinate to a main one so that *but* joins two main clauses:

> He was a doctor with many good qualities but *he was unpopular.*

The rule that conjunctions link grammatical units of equal value should be carefully followed when using such expressions as *but which*, *and which*, *and who*, etc.

See **and which, clause 1, 3, conjunction.**

C

can. It is correct to make a distinction between *can* (=*have the (physical) ability to* do something) and *may* (=*have permission to* do something): thus *Can you call this evening?* but *May I call this evening?* The distinction is illustrated by this exchange during a grammar lesson:

> Child (to teacher): Please miss, can I leave the room?
> Teacher: You can, but you may not.

However, in informal English the distinction is increasingly ignored. See **may.**

can't seem is widely used in such expressions as

> I can't seem to find it.

A moment's thought will show that

> I seem unable to find it.

is more logical. *I can't seem to . . .* makes sense in some contexts, but not many.

See **appear.**

cant, apart from meaning *hypocrisy*, means the peculiar language of a profession, sect or class, especially the private language of criminals. The more common word is now **jargon.**

canvas, the cloth, should not be confused with *canvass* (verb and noun), which has to do with the ascertaining of opinion.

capital letter. A capital letter is used

1. at the beginning of a sentence. See also **direct speech, interjection.**

2. for proper nouns. See **noun 1.**

3. for the important words in the titles of books, films, etc.
4. for the word *I* and when addressing relatives: *Auntie Jane, Grandpa.*
5. for words connected with religion: *God, the Bible, the Anglican Church.*

capitalism is pronounced with the emphasis on the first syllable, not the second.

captivate, **capture**. The former means *charm, fascinate, overpower with excellence*; the latter means *take prisoner*. The advertising-copy writer who composed

> When people pick up one of the books, they are *captured* by its clarity and style

seeems to have confused the two (unless he intended to use *capture* in a non-literal sense, in which case the metaphor is inappropriately over-emphatic).

case. 1. In the sense of *state of affairs*, *case* is over-used. Note the following possibilities:

> It is the case that . . . (It is true that . . .)
> That is not the case. (That is not so.)
> Less difficulty is expected than was the case when . . .
> (than occured when . . .)
> In many cases, his answers were . . . (Many of his answers were . . .)

The expression *in the case of* can often be omitted from a sentence without loss of sense.

The word has many legitimate uses, but its over-use is a common fault, a cause of monotony and a sign of laziness in the writer. See **instance**.

2. Some grammar books use the word *case* to describe the relationship between:

(*a*) a noun or pronoun and a verb, i.e. whether a noun or pronoun is the subject (or *nominative case*) or the object (*accusative case*) of a verb.

(*b*) a noun or pronoun and a preposition. The main rule here is that a preposition is followed by a pronoun in the accusative:

> It was addressed *to* my husband and *me*.

(*c*) a noun or pronoun and another noun when the former is expressing possession, i.e. it is in the *genitive case*:

> *birds'* nests; *our* holidays.

In this dictionary, the term *possessive* is used instead of *genitive*.

catalyst

The terms *nominative* and *accusative* have little significance in English except in the understanding of pronouns, which are the only words which have different forms depending on whether they are acting as the subject of verbs or the object of verbs and prepositions.

catalyst. In chemistry, catalysis is the effect produced by a substance that aids a chemical change in other bodies without undergoing change itself. A *catalyst* is an agent in this change. The word has become a popular metaphor, illustrated by the following quotations from the same issue of a newspaper:

> They saw themselves as catalysts changing individuals
> and eventually society to a simpler style of living based
> on less materialism.
> One of the central elements of his technique is the use of
> players who, for want of a less hackneyed term, could
> be called catalysts (*in inspiring other players to better
> performance*).

As the writer of the latter sentence acknowledges by his use of 'hackneyed', popular metaphors may rapidly turn into clichés. Moreover, their original, precise meaning may be lost sight of, or be unknown to those who enjoy using fashionable expressions without finding out what they mean. The consequence may be the sort of absurd mixed metaphor quoted by Gowers: *a catalyst for a ferment of change, a catalyst for bridging the gap*. Like all near-clichés, *catalyst* should be used sparingly, and always with respect for its original meaning.

catholic: universal, of wide sympathies, broad-minded, tolerant. It is usually applied to a person's tastes or interests. The *Catholic Church* is the universal body of Christians. To use *Catholic Church* when meaning *Roman Catholic Church*, or to use *Catholics* instead of *Roman Catholics*, is therefore offensive to many Christians of other denominations, which would claim that since the Reformation the Roman Church has had no exclusive right to apply the single word *catholic* to itself.

cause. See **due to**.

censor as a verb means *exercise censorship* and should not be confused with *censure* as a verb, which means *blame, reprove, criticise unfavourably*.

centre is more precise than *middle*, and is not used of time (*the middle of the night*) or linear extension (*the middle of the road*). The *middle* of the floor is the space around its *centre* (Partridge).

centre (a)round is incorrect, although it is probably more frequently used than the correct *centre on*. A moment's thought will show that

26

something cannot centre *around* something else, only *on* it. In mathematical and other precise contexts, *centre in* may be used; so may *centre at*, meaning *place the centre at*. But never *centre around*, the popularity of which probably results from confusion with the (correct) use *revolve around*. The following, from the *Cambridge Students' Prospectus, 1978*, illustrates the error:

> Its social life centres round a large, rather squalid bar.

change has the adjective *changeable*.

charisma should not be used as if it meant no more than *popularity* or *attractiveness*. It meant, originally, a grace bestowed by God, and has come to mean a special and inexplicable quality of personality that sets a man apart and enables him to exercise leadership or exceptional influence. The word therefore means something rare and important, and should not be cheapened by being made a substitute for mere *glamour*.

check out is an Americanism and an unnecessary elaboration of *check* (in the sense of *examine or re-examine the accuracy of*) as in

> The police are checking out reports that the wanted
> man has been seen in Gateshead.

The expression has probably come to stay in its sense of *pay one's bill and leave*.

childish is to be distinguished from *childlike*: the former is a derogatory term meaning *puerile, immature, improper for a grown person*; the latter is not derogatory, and means *having good qualities of a child, as innocence, frankness, etc.*

chronic means *lingering, lasting, inveterate*, and its widespread use to mean *intense, severe, bad* is distinctly slangy.

From this slang use derives the belief that *chronic* means the same as *acute* when applied to serious disease, pain, shortage, inability, etc. On the contrary, *acute* here means *coming sharply to a crisis*, which is the very opposite of *chronic*. There are thus important differences between *chronic shortage, acute shortage* and *severe shortage*.

circle round, as in

> The crash occurred while several aircraft were circling
> round, waiting to land.

is an example of **tautology**, the adverb *round* being obviously unnecessary with *circle*.

circumstances. It has been argued that the common expression *under the circumstances* is incorrect, because circumstances are around us, not above us. *In the circumstances* is always correct, therefore, but few would quarrel with *under the circumstances* if the expression is used to suggest pressure. In other contexts, use *in the circumstances*.

claim, as a verb, means *demand as one's due*, as in
> Those who wish to claim the new supplementary
> benefit should apply immediately.

It is an unnecessary weakening of a precise word to use it as a substitute for *state* or *assert*.

Similarly, as a noun, a *claim* is a right (not a statement) or a demand for something as a right (not a mere request).

class is a singular noun and needs the singular *this* or *that*.
> The public is interested in watching those class of
> cricketers.

should have *that class*.

classic, classical. As adjectives, both mean *of the first class*. The latter however, is normally applied to works of art and their creators. With a capital letter it refers to ancient Greece and Rome.

clause. A group of words containing a finite verb (i.e. a verb with a subject; see **verb 3**).

1. In the sentence
> They *abandoned* the ascent when snow *began* to fall

there are two finite verbs (italicised) and thus two clauses:
> 1. They abandoned the ascent
> 2. when snow began to fall

The second clause is dependent on the first: it does not make sense without it. The first clause, which makes complete sense on its own, is called the *main clause*. The second, which does not make complete sense on its own, is called a *subordinate* (or dependent) clause.

(For other examples of main clauses, see **sentence**.)

2. A subordinate clause is part of a sentence. It can do the work of an adjective, adverb or noun.

(*a*) An adjectival clause is a group of words containing a finite verb and doing the work of an adjective in describing a noun or pronoun in the main clause:
> Where is the glove (*which*) *you bought yesterday*?
> He *who hesitates* is lost.

(*b*) An adverbial clause does the work of an adverb in telling more about the verb in the main clause.
> They were overjoyed *when the news arrived*.

The italicised subordinate clause states *the time* when the verb in the main clause took place.

Memories haunted him *wherever he went.*

The adverbial clause states *the place* where he was *haunted.*

The drought lasted so long *that the stream ran dry.*

The subordinate clause gives *the result* of the action of the verb in the main clause.

The tourists left *because revolution broke out.*

The clause gives *the reason* for the verb in the main clause.

If you drive fast, you'll get there tonight, *unless there's a lot of traffic.*

The two subordinate adverbial clauses both state the conditions under which the action of the main verb will occur.

Stand on the wall *so that you may see better.*

The subordinate clause states *the purpose* or result of the main verb *Stand.* See **in order that, may.**

(c) A noun clause does the work of a noun in acting as the subject, object or complement of the verb in the main clause:

How it happened will never be known. (subject)

He insisted *that the dog had menaced him.* (object)

That is *what I expected.* (complement)

3. A common grammatical error occurs when linking a subordinate clause to a main clause by using a conjunction followed by a pronoun (*and who, and which, but whose,* etc.). A conjunction can only be used when linking grammatical units of the same kind (see **conjunction**). In the sentence

He was a man of great wisdom and whose charm everyone admired.

the conjunction *and* is joining a phrase (*of great wisdom*) and a clause (*whose charm everyone admired*). This is not possible, because a phrase and a clause are not of the same grammatical kind. To correct the sentence, either omit the conjunction, thus avoiding the problem of grammatical equivalence,

He was a man of great wisdom whose charm everyone admired.

or turn the phrase *of great wisdom* into a clause so that the conjunction links two clauses:

He was a man who had great wisdom and whose charm everyone admired.

4. For an explanation of the difference between clauses which describe and those which define, see **that.**

5. Note the same clause can have different functions:

I don't know *when the train is due*. (noun clause, object
of *know* in the main clause)
Do you know the time *when the train is due*? (adjectival
clause describing the noun *time*)
Call me *when the train is due*. (adverbial clause saying
more about the verb *Call* in the main clause)
6. When punctuating clauses, commas are to be used with care.
I'm not playing tennis because it's raining.
implies that I am playing tennis for some other reason.
I'm not playing tennis, because it's raining.
is quite unambiguous.

cliché. An over-used expression, so hackneyed as to be both a tired substitute for original thought and an offence to the intelligence of the
reader or listener. Clichés are often found in the speeches of politicians
and the utterances of sports reporters, but other examples abound:
*the moment of truth, stand up and be counted, last but not least, in this day
and age, gallant loser, at this moment in time, slowly but surely, conspicuous
by his absence.* Cliché may also occur in drama, film, music, etc., in
the form of any outworn piece of technique.

collaborate. See **tautology**.

collect. See **tautology**.

collective noun. See **noun 2, pronoun 8 (b)**.

colloquialism. The *colloquial* is the language one normally uses in informal contexts, at home or with friends, as distinct from the more
formal English one uses in business letters, speeches, examinations, etc.
Colloquialisms therefore belong to the body of language between
Standard English and **slang**.

colon. The colon (:) has the following uses within a sentence.
1. To introduce a list:
I can think of four reasons for not going to Yugoslavia:
the distance, the cost, the food, and the people.
Not all lists are introduced by a colon, only those where punctuation is needed to indicate a pause. A colon would be wrong in
The loft was filled with old furniture, discarded toys,
several carpets and a bed.
because no pause is needed after *with*.
2. To separate two balancing halves of a sentence:
The first battle had been a disaster: the second was
unmitigated catastrophe.

In such cases the colon must be placed between main clauses (see **clause 1**) which 'balance' in the sense that they are of similar construction.

3. To indicate that what follows the colon amplifies or explains what precedes it:

> Much would depend on the outcome of the election: either the nationalist party would be proved right, or it could be expected to cease to exist as a credible political force.

Here, the words after the colon amplify *much*.

comma. Commas are used to divide up sentences to make them more easily understood. They are equivalent to slight pauses in speech.

They are normally used

1. to mark off phrases:

> *Messiah*, Handel's finest oratorio, was composed in 1742.
> Far from being a day of rest, Sunday is busier than a week-day.

When two commas are used round a phrase, as in the first example, they are rather like brackets, and it is as wrong to use only one comma in such circumstances as it would be to open brackets and fail to close them:

> The roof was, in the builder's opinion likely to cave in.
> The roof was in the builder's opinion, likely to cave in.

The main sense here is

> The roof was likely to cave in

and the phrase *in the builder's opinion* is inserted; it should have commas before and after it.

> See also **verb 5 (b)**.

2. to mark off clauses, if the sense requires pauses:

> The lumberjack, who was quite nonplussed, fell silent.

See also **clause 2, sentence 3, 4** and the section on absolute construction under **verb 5 (b) iii**.

3. when someone is addressed:

> Will you please come in, Mr Anderson?

4. when several items are listed:

> A brass bedstead, a tin bath, an old gas cooker and several mattresses fell off the lorry.

A comma is optional before the final conjunction in such a list:

> We bought eggs, asparagus, milk, and a week's supply of budgerigar-seed.

See **8** below.

5. The most common misuse of the comma is to use it as a link between two sentences:

The price of tobacco has gone up, this is the third
increase in two years.

The only punctuation that can link two sentences is the **semi-colon** or the **colon**. Either a semi-colon (to link) or a full stop (to separate) would have been correct instead of a comma in the above example.

If a sentence consists of more than two main clauses (see **clause 1**), of which the final two are linked by a conjunction, a comma may link the others:

Beat the eggs, add the cream and mix them together.

A full explanation of such constructions is given under **sentence 3**.

In such sentences, a comma would not be incorrect before the final conjunction, and may indeed be necessary to reinforce it by drawing attention to some change of direction in the sentence:

The base should be laid first, then the walls should be
screwed in place, but the door frame should not be
added until the roof is in position.

6. A sentence may have its meaning considerably changed by the insertion of a comma. Compare

Children dislike teachers who show favouritism.
Children dislike teachers, who show favouritism.

The first means that children dislike *only those* teachers who show favouritism; it implies that they may like other teachers who do not. The second sentence means that *all* teachers show favouritism and that *all* are disliked by children.

All Londoners who are born within the sound of Bow
Bells are called cockneys.
All Londoners, who are born within the sound of Bow
Bells, are called cockneys.

The second means

All Londoners are called cockneys

and the rest of the sentence, inserted between two commas, is a description of all Londoners. This is obviously not what the writer intended to say, because it is not true.

These examples point an important difference between clauses that *describe* and those that *define*. This difference is dealt with under **that**. Describing clauses need commas; defining clauses do not. Note the differences between

They serve beer which I don't like. (defining)
They serve beer, which I don't like. (describing)

The lad who delivers our papers is always punctual.
(defining)
The boy, who is unemployed, was placed on probation.
(describing)

7. It is sometimes said that words such as *however, perhaps, therefore,* etc., must always be enclosed in commas. This is not so: commas are needed only if such words need to be emphasised by pauses before and after them.

8. When a sentence lists a number of items, with the normal pattern of

—, —, — and —

it is essential that the items indicated by — are of equal grammatical status (see definition of **conjunction**).

He grows fruit, vegetables, and keeps pigs.

is therefore unacceptable (because *fruit* and *vegetables* are nouns, while *(he) keeps pigs* is a clause). The reader is led to expect a noun after *and*, and the introduction of a different construction is ungrammatical. The sentence should read

He grows fruit and vegetables, and keeps pigs.

which now consists of two sentences

He grows fruit and vegetables.
He keeps pigs.

correctly joined by a conjunction, according to the pattern described under **sentence 3**.

commence(ment) is formal; in most circumstances, *begin(ning)* or *start* suffices.

commit is spelt so. Note commit*t*ed, commit*t*ing, but commi*t*ment.

committee may be singular or plural. Use a singular verb when the sense of unity is intended (e.g. *The committee meets monthly*), and a plural verb when the opposite sense is required (e.g. *The committee are in disagreement*) or when the emphasis is on the individual members rather than on their corporate identity. See **noun 2**.

common noun. See **noun**.

common sense should be written as two words. A hyphen should be used for the adjectival form (*a common-sense attitude*).

communal should be pronounced with the emphasis on the first syllable.

compact has the stress on the first syllable when the word is used as

comparable

a noun meaning *agreement*. In the other senses (e.g. as adjective meaning *closely packed together*) the stress is on the second syllable.

comparable has the accent on the first syllable, not the second.

comparative, comparison are spelt so. The former is often wrongly spelt with *-it-* instead of *-at-*.

comparative degree. See **adjective 1, adverb 2 (a)**.

comparatively is often used unnecessarily. It should be used only when a standard of comparison has been stated or implied.

    They live in a comparatively large house.

means that the house is large in comparison with other houses, but *large* means precisely that without the aid of *comparatively*, which is either redundant, or incorrect for *fairly*.

    Comparatively few holiday-makers come at Easter.

means not that few holiday-makers come, but that their numbers are smaller than those at other periods of the year. This is a legitimate use of *comparatively*, and the sense of the sentence would be changed by its omission.

    Note that *a comparatively few* is wrong: the noun *few* needs an adjective (*a very few*), not an adverb.

compare, contrast. The former means *estimate the similarity of*, the latter *show the difference between*. Both words are normally followed by *with*. *Compare to* means *liken to*.

comparison has an i, *comparative* an a.

comparison with, not *comparison to*, especially in the phrase *in comparison with*.

complement: full number required (to complete). Thus *the train's complement of passengers*. Not to be confused with *compliment*, which means *expression of praise*. Remember the difference by noting the relationship between *complement* and *complete*, both of which have *-ple-*.

    For *complement* as part of a sentence, see **verb 4, 7; pronoun 1 (b)**.

complex, as a noun, is a fashionable substitute for *collection* (e.g. a *complex of reasons*) and is best reserved to denote an entity of which the parts or their arrangement are complicated. See also **inferiority complex**.

compliment. See **complement**.

component part. *Component* = contributing to the composition of a whole. *Part* = some but not all of a thing or number of things. These two words are used together so frequently that one is bound to ask if *part* can never be used on its own. It can, and ought to be; the adjective *component* should not be used unless it adds meaning.

compound does *not* mean *worsen*, despite its very frequent and erroneous use in such contexts as

> The tribunal's error of judgment was compounded by their failure to call all the witnesses who wished to give evidence.

The error arises from a misunderstanding of the legal expression *compound a felony*, which means *refrain from prosecution on private motives*. It does not mean *make an offence worse*. *Compound* normally means *combine*.

As a verb, the word is pronounced with the stress on the second syllable: as a noun or adjective it has the stress on the first syllable.

comprise. *Comprise of* is wrong. Not

> The concert will comprise of two symphonies.

but simply

> The concert will comprise two symphonies.

The error probably stems from confusion with *consist of*, which is correct and means the same as *comprise*.

A common version of the same error is seen in

> The film was comprised of research material.

Instead of *comprised*, the word *constituted* (i.e. made up) should have been used.

Note that, since *comprise* = consist of (certain elements), it is correct to say

> The concert comprises two symphonies.

but not

> Two symphonies comprise the concert.

conducive should be followed by *to*, not *of*.

conjunction. A word which acts as a link between words or groups of words when the words (e.g. two nouns, two adverbs, etc.) or groups of words (two phrases, clauses or sentences) are grammatical equivalents:

> Phone on Monday *or* Wednesday. (two nouns)
> Let's get home *before* the rain starts. (two sentences)
> *Although* he was limping, he kept going. (two sentences)

35

He is a man who says little *but* (who) thinks deeply.
(two clauses)

It must be remembered that a phrase can do the work of a noun, adjective or adverb, thus acting as the 'equivalent' of one of them. A conjunction can thus link, for example, an adverb and an adverbial phrase:

She spoke *slowly* and *with deep feeling.*

Words which are used as conjunctions in some contexts can be used as other parts of speech in other contexts:

What have you been doing *since* we last met?
(conjunction, linking two sentences)
The building has *since* been demolished. (adverb, telling when the action of the verb *demolished* took place)
They haven't met *since* Christmas. (preposition, expressing the relationship between the noun *Christmas* and the clause *They haven't met*).

It used to be said that one should never begin a sentence with the conjunctions *and* or *but*. No-one would now regard this rule as valid. To begin a sentence with *And* is a useful way of adding emphasis: it has the effect of underlining the *And*. This device, however, is weakened if it is used too much.

connexion. The spelling *connection* is also found. See **regard**.

consensus means *agreement of opinion* (or of evidence). The common phrase the *consensus of opinion* is therefore nonsensical, meaning *the agreement of opinion of opinion. Consensus* suffices on its own. See **tautology**.

One may *seek, find* or *reach* a consensus: one may not *take a consensus*. Consensus has nothing to do with *census*.

The spelling *concensus* is wrong.

consequent (up)on, not *consequent to. Consequent* means *resulting*, and should not be confused with *subsequent*, which means *following*, and which is sometimes used where *consequent* would be more exact.

Consequential is used only in legal phraseology and means *resulting indirectly* (as in *consequential damages*). In other contexts, *consequential* means *self-important*.

School closures will be consequential on the fall in birth-rate.

should therefore have *consequent on*.

consequential. See **consequent**.

considerable is so heavily used as an all-purpose adjective that its omission would probably strengthen rather than weaken such common expressions as *considerable doubt, considerable risk, a considerable number of, considerable delay, etc.*

considering. See **verb 10**.

consist. See **comprise**.

consonant: any letter of the alphabet other than a **vowel**. The letter *h*, however, usually a consonant, as in *house*, is sometimes silent, as in *hour*. The letter *y* is a consonant, though it may sometimes act as a vowel (*myself, rhythm*). See also **syllable**.

constitute. See **comprise**.

contagious, applied to disease, means *spread by physical contact* with a person or thing. *Infectious* means *liable to be transmitted by air or water*.

containerise and *containerisation* are recently invented words having to do with the packing and carrying of goods in large, sealed containers instead of in smaller and more numerous packages. The words are typical of many new words formed by adding *-ise* and *-isation* to existing words. Some of these newly coined words (neologisms) are well established and useful (*publicise, finalise, computerise*); others are less acceptable (*hospitalise, randomise*); some are too hideous to quote. Usage will determine which of these will finally deserve to appear in dictionaries, but there is never any justification for a neologism unless it is significantly more useful than an existing word or phrase. *Hospitalisation*, for instance, saves neither breath, ink nor time compared with *sending to hospital*, and is uglier.

contemptible: deserving of contempt. *Contemptuous*: full of contempt.

contest, as a noun, is pronounced with the emphasis on the first syllable. As a verb, it is pronounced with the stress on the second syllable.

continual: always going on; very frequent; thought of as never coming to an end (Fowler). *Continuous*: connected, unbroken; uninterrupted in time or sequence; with no break between the beginning and the not necessarily long-deferred end (Fowler).

> Continuous work is impossible if there are continual interruptions.

Water may flow *continously*, but a tap drips *continually*.

continue to remain is an example of **tautology**.

> He continues to remain in good health.

should be either

> He continues in good health.

or

      He remains in good health.

continuous tense. See **verb 2**.

contrast, as a verb, is pronounced with the accent on the second syllable. As a noun, it has the accent on the first. See **compare**.

controversy is pronounced with the emphasis on the first syllable, not the second. In the forms *controversial* and *controversially* the accent is on the third syllable.

co-operate and **cooperate** are both correct, as are *co-operation, cooperation*, etc. The forms without the hyphen are slightly more common. See **together**.
    Avoid *cooperate together* and *mutual cooperation*. See **mutual, tautology**.

correspond. It is safest to reserve *correspond with* to mean *exchange letters with*, and in all other cases to use *correspond to*.

could is the past tense of *can* (*We could not afford a holiday last year*), but may also be used
    1. as a verb in the present tense to mean *feel inclined to*:
        I could kick myself for forgetting.
    2. as a slightly gentler substitute for *can*:
        Could you direct me to the post-office?

council and **counsel** must be differentiated. The former means *assembly of people* (*municipal council, council of war*). The latter means *advice* (*take my counsel*) and is also applied to a barrister (*take counsel's opinion*). *Councillor* is usually confined to local government; a *counsellor* is one who gives advice (*marriage-guidance counsellor*).

counter-productive. Producing an effect opposite to (not merely different from) that which is desirable. The word is too much used as a loose alternative to *unprofitable, detrimental*, etc.

court-martial. The plural is *courts-martial*. See also **handful**.

credence, meaning *belief*, is sometimes confused with *credibility* (the quality of being credible, i.e. believable). *Credence* is wrongly used in
        The trial will be public, in an attempt to give some
        credence to the President's insistence that he has nothing
        to hide.

It is correctly used in
> It is impossible to give any credence to the President's
> version of events.

credibility is believability, the quality of being believable. Its adjective is *credible*, meaning *believable* (a *credible story*). There is sometimes confusion between this and *creditable* (meaning *bringing credit*: a creditable performance is one that reflects credit on the performer) and *credulous* (meaning *believing too readily, easily fooled*). See **credence**.

credible. See **credibility**.

credulity is over-readiness to believe anything. It is sometimes confused with *credence* (belief) as it is in
> Reports of the damage were so sensational that the
> government refused to give them any credulity.

The adjective is *credulous* (believing too readily; easily fooled), the opposite of which is *incredulous* (filled with disbelief). See **credence, credibility**.

credulous. See **credulity** and **credibility**.

crisis has the plural *crises* (pronounced crise-ees).

criteria is the plural of *criterion*, not, as is often thought, the singular form. It is therefore wrong to speak of *a criteria* or *the criteria is* … One criterion, several criteria.

curb, as a noun, is usually found in its sense of *restraint* (*a curb on spending*); as a verb, it means *restrain* (*he has difficulty in curbing his enthusiasm*). In the sense of *footpath-edging*, the spelling *kerb* is normal.

curricula is the plural of *curriculum* and should not be confused with the adjectival *curricular*: a school's extra-*curricular* activities are those which are not part of the curriculum.

D

dare has the past tense *dared* (usually *did not dare* in negative uses). The past tense *durst* is not incorrect but it is now seldom found.

dash. The dash (–) must be distinguished from the **hyphen**. The hyphen links words: the dash separates groups of words. The dash always indicates a slight pause.

datum

1. The dash is used most characteristically to introduce a summary or amplification:

> The book is the product of collaboration by authors, researchers, photographers and designers – a team of thirty in all.

2. It may also introduce and conclude an explanatory parenthesis, as may brackets:

> According to the report, there are more absent-minded women than men – 12% of the population, as against 10% in the case of men – but the report is unable to explain this difference.

3. The dash may also be used when a sentence (e.g. a piece of **direct speech**) is interrupted or left unfinished, or when the writer wishes to introduce an anticipatory pause before a surprising or humorous statement or a climax:

> You'll never guess what he won – an electric carving-knife!

4. The dash should not be used as an all-purpose punctuation mark replacing much other punctuation, as it often was in printed books (especially of the last century) and as it still is used by some modern writers.

datum has the plural *data*, which is often incorrectly used as if it were singular (e.g. *the data is* ... instead of *the data are* ...). Data are things known, from which inferences may be drawn. The first syllable rhymes with *day*.

day and age, in this. An over-used expression, now becoming deservedly recognised as a resounding cliché, to be avoided at all costs. Say *nowadays, at present,* or *now*.

deadly silence should be *deathly silence*. *Deathly*: like death. Deadly: extremely (*deadly dull*) or extremely accurate and damaging (*the left-arm spinner's deadly bowling*), though there are other meanings. *Silence, hush,* etc., clearly need *deathly*.

dearth. Protesting at an advertising campaign, the writer of a letter to a newspaper referred to *the recent dearth of full-page advertisements*. Since *dearth* means *scarcity*, he had the wrong word; perhaps the word he had vaguely in mind was *plethora* (unhealthy excess). It is an unusual mistake, but a useful illustration of the rule that the common word one is sure of is safer than the slightly more showy word which has not yet been confidently absorbed into one's vocabulary.

decade is pronounced with the emphasis on the first syllable.

decided, decisive. The former means *unquestionable* (*a decided preference*; *a decidedly wrong decision*). The latter means *conclusive*, i.e. deciding some issue, or going far towards deciding it (*a decisive victory*). A decisive person is one who makes up his mind quickly and clearly, and then acts to bring about some result.

defective, deficient. The former should be used to mean *faulty*, the latter to mean *lacking* or *incomplete*. There are occasions when either word will do (e.g. when a fault and a lack are inseparable) but if a distinction exists it should be reflected in the correct choice of word.

definite is often mis-spelt *definate*. See also **definitive**.

Both *definite* and *definitely* are very often used in sentences to which they add no meaning. *Definite* means *precise, distinct, with exact limits*. It weakens expression if it is used as an all-purpose intensive. There is no point in saying *I definitely think* if all that one means is *I think*.

definite article is the grammatical description of the word *the*. It is pronounced *thee* before a **vowel** and a silent *h*; otherwise it is pronounced in the normal way before a **consonant** or before a vowel which is a *yoo* sound as in *universe, euphoria*, etc.

See **a, an**.

definitive: final (*a definitive answer*). A *definitive* study is the 'last word' on a subject. *Definitive* should not be confused with **definite**, which means *precise*.

degree. The common phrase *to a less degree* should be used when two things are being referred to, because *less* is the comparative form (see **adjective 1, 3**):

> Male cosmetics are widely used in America, and to a less degree in England.

Lesser means *less than less*, and *to a lesser degree* should not be used unless this is the intended sense. See **less, lesser.**

The expression *to a more or less degree* is bad English because, though *a less degree* makes sense, *a more degree* does not.

delusion, illusion. A delusion is a *fixed* false impression, a firm belief that what is false is true, e.g. as a symptom or form of madness. One speaks of *delusions of grandeur* or of *labouring under a delusion*.

An *illusion* is rather more pleasant, less fixed and less likely to show itself in behaviour. It is a *false impression, conception or idea*, a *deceptive belief, statement or appearance*. A conjuror's tricks are, and a politician's promises may be, *illusions*.

Those who discover that their illusions are false become *disillusioned*: those whose delusions are ended are *undeceived*, though these two verbs are interchangeable in practice.

demur, demure. The former is a noun or verb, and rhymes with *occur*: the latter is an adjective, and rhymes with *pure*.

Demur (verb): make difficulties, raise scruples or objections, take exception.

If that is your intention, I must demur.

Demur (noun): objection

The plan has been accepted without demur.

Demure (adjective): composed, grave, affectedly coy; serious; reserved in demeanour.

An occasional error is to use the adjective instead of the verb:

The management has drawn up a set of proposals, but the shop-stewards are expected to demure.

deny does not mean the same as *refute*.

Deny: declare that something is untrue.

Refute: prove that something is untrue.

depend. It is colloquial to say *It depends whether* ..., and better to write *It depends (up)on whether* ...

dependant, dependent. It is best to retain the former for use as a noun meaning *one who depends on another for support*, and the latter for adjectival use:

In certain circumstances, one may claim tax relief on expenditure to support dependants.

The rate of relief is dependent on one's income.

deprecate, depreciate. The former means *strongly disapprove of*. The latter means *diminish in value* (i.e. the opposite of *appreciate*):

The plan to build a motorway close to the village is to be deprecated. Houses in the area will depreciate sharply.

depth. The fashionable phrase *in depth* (*an in-depth study*, *an examination in depth*) is in danger of ousting *careful*, *long* and *detailed* from the language, and does not deserve to do so.

derisive, derisory. The former means *conveying derision* (ridicule, mockery) as in *a derisive cheer*. The latter means *inviting or worthy of derision* as in *a derisory offer*.

despatch is correct, but *dispatch* is now much more normal.

detract, distract. The former is usually found in *detract from*, meaning *take away from, depreciate*:
> The scenery detracted from the performance.

i.e. reduced the credit due to the performance.

Distract means *divert or confuse* (attention), *bewilder, perplex*:
> The scenery distracted the audience.

i.e. drew the audience's attention away from the performance.

Detract is usually intransitive, *distract* usually transitive (see **verb 4, 6**).

develop, development should be so spelt, without an *e* after the *p*.

device, devise. *Device* is the noun. *Devise* (pronounced *-ize*) is the verb.

devil's advocate. A misunderstood expression. It does not mean *someone who defends the devil* (in the sense of an unpopular person or cause), but someone who points out the faults in a respected person or a good cause, not necessarily because he believes the faults outweigh the goodness, but perhaps because he wishes to be impartial or to ensure balanced discussion.

dice. See **die**.

didn't ought is wrong, as in *You didn't ought to have done it.* The correct versions are *You ought not to have done it* or *You should not have done it.*

die (noun) is seldom found except in the common expressions *the die is cast* (an irrevocable decision has been taken) and *straight as a die* (very straight). Its plural is *dice* which is often incorrectly used (e.g. in the printed instructions to games of chance) as if it were singular.

differ from is always safe. *Differ with* is permissible, but uncommon, when the meaning is *disagree with*. *Differ from* is more usual, and is always necessary when the meaning is *be different*. See **different from**.

different from is correct; *different than* is not, except in America. *Different to* is becoming common, but since the verb *differ* is always followed by *from*, never *to*, when it means *be different*, there is no good reason for not insisting likewise on *different from*.
See **differ from, differently**.

differently is the adverb formed from the adjective *different*.
> Things were different when I was a boy.

is correct: *different* describes the noun *Things*. Also correct is
> Things were done differently when I was a boy.

where the adverb *differently* is needed to describe the verb *were done*, i.e. to describe *how* things *were done*.

It is an error to use *different* when *differently* is required, as in
> Children nowadays learn French different from the way
> I was taught.

They may learn *a different sort* of French, but they *learn differently*.

dilemma has a useful and precise meaning: a dilemma is a *position that leaves a choice between two* (or at least a definite number of) *equal evils*. There is no good reason for using it loosely to mean any sort of difficulty or problem.

diphthong (pronounced dif-thong). Two vowels pronounced in one syllable (*round*ly, *spoil*ing) or forming a single vowel-sound (d*ea*d, gr*ou*p).

direct object. See **verb 4.**

direct speech consists of a speaker's or writer's actual words or thoughts:
> Shakespeare wrote, 'Neither a borrower nor a lender
> be.'
> 'Why do people choose to live in cities?' he thought.

For the rules of punctuation of direct speech, see **quotation marks**.

disagree is best followed by *with*, not *from*.

disaster, but *disastrous* (not *-erous*).

disinterest does not mean *lack of interest*. It means *impartiality*.
> He shows a complete disinterest in his studies.

is wrong. People who should show *disinterest* are judges, referees, examiners, etc., in that they are not 'interested parties', seeking to show favour or serve their own self-interest. In the above example, *disinterest* should have been *lack of interest*.

Disinterest is much misunderstood and misused, and its correct definition should be carefully observed. See **disinterested**.

disinterested is very often confused with *uninterested* (which is the opposite of *interested*).

Disinterested: not biased by self-seeking; impartial.

Uninterested: lacking in interest, concern or curiosity.

A football referee should be *disinterested*; he need not necessarily be *uninterested* in the game.

The sort of misuse exemplified by
> He is disinterested in politics.

which is intended to mean

He is uninterested (*or* not interested) in politics.

is one of the most common grammatical errors in English.

distinctive: *serving to distinguish* (as in *distinctive uniform*; police cars of a *distinctive colour*). Not to be confused with *distinct*, meaning *clear* (*a distinct improvement*), *separate* (*four distinct parts*), etc.

divergent. Going in different directions from each other or from a common point. The word implies an irreconcilability which is not contained in the weaker *different*. There is an important distinction between *divergent opinions* and *different opinions*.

double negative. This may be a legitimate literary device:

The result was *not un*expected.

It is *not* that we are *un*grateful.

These sentences have a hint of reservation which is not found in

The result was expected.

We are grateful.

It is almost as if the double negative forms lead the reader to expect the sentences to continue *but* . . . .

Care must be taken, however, to ensure that the double negative is not wrongly used, as it is in

I do*n't* know *no*thing about it.

He could*n't* find it *no*where.

These, grammatically, say the opposite of what is intended: if one does *not* know nothing, one knows something. One negative (italicised) should have been omitted. See **negatives**.

doubt(ful) should be followed by *that* (occasionally *but that*) if a sentence is in the negative or the interrogative:

I don't doubt that . . .

Is there any doubt that . . . ?

Otherwise it should be followed by *whether*, though *if* is increasingly found.

dramatic irony occurs in a play or story when there arises a situation the significance of which has been revealed to the spectator or reader, but not to the characters in the play or story.

dream has either *dreamt* or *dreamed* as past tense and past participle: *dreamt* is the more common.

drink has the past tense *drank* and the past participle *drunk* (i.e. *have/ has/had drunk*). The adjective is *drunken* when it is attached to a noun

drunk, drunken

(*drunken behaviour*, *drunken people*), and *drunk* when used on its own (*He is/became/was drunk* etc.).

drunk, drunken. See **drink**.

dry has the forms *drier, driest, dried, drily*; but *dryness* and *drying*.

due to. *Due* is an adjective, except when used to refer to the points of the compass: *Go due* (i.e. exactly) *west*. (In this case it is an adverb.) It means *attributable*. *Due to* = caused by. Like all adjectives, it needs a noun to go with it.

> His bad temper is due to the heat.

is correct.

> Due to the rain, the match was cancelled.

is incorrect because, grammatically, the adjective *due* describes the noun (*match*), and the match was not *due to the rain*. The intention of the sentence is to apply the adjectival *due to the rain* to the verb *cancelled*, but this is impossible because adjectives do not describe verbs.

> The cancellation was due to the rain.

is correct, because the adjectival *due* is properly related to a noun, *cancellation*.

Care must always be taken to use the adjectival *due to* only when it can be correctly related to a noun. If it cannot, use *owing to* or *because of* instead.

The expression *due to* is used incorrectly in the following sentences:

> The reason for the cancellation was due to the rain.
> The cause of the fault was due to over-heating.

The reason was not due to the rain: the reason *was* the rain. Omit either *The reason for* or *due to*.

Similarly, because *due to* means *caused by*, the second sentence means

> The cause of the fault was caused by over-heating.

The correct versions are

> The cause of the fault was over-heating.
> The fault was due to over-heating.

If in doubt, use *owing to* or *because of*, which can be used in all circumstances, because they do not suffer from the limitations imposed by the exclusively adjectival nature of *due to*. See **owing to**.

E

each, when the subject of a verb, is singular, and must have a singular verb:

> Each of them *was* busy.

Care must be taken to ensure that any subsequent pronoun referring to *each* is also singular:

> Each of them (*or* us) was busy with *his* work.

Note that *his* does duty for *his or her*. It is quite wrong to say

> Each of them was busy with *their* work.

each other. It used to be taught that *each other* was to be used of two persons or things, and *one another* of more than two. By this rule, *They hated each other* indicated that two people were involved; *They hated one another* referred to more than two people.

The rule never had much validity or use, and is now usually ignored.

easier is the comparative form of the adjective *easy*; the alternative form is *more easy* (see **adjective 1**). It is *not* the comparative form of the adverb *easily*, which is *more easily*. The common expression *Take it easy* is actually incorrect, since *easy* is an adjective and the phrase requires the adverb *easily*, describing *how* 'it' should be *taken* (see **adverb 1**). The expression is doubtless here to stay, but *easier* as an adverb should be avoided in other contexts. Thus

> The job can be done easier if you have the right tools.

should have *more easily*, the adverb being necessary to describe the verb *can be done*.

eatable. See **inedible**.

economic should not be confused with *economical*, which means *thrifty*, *cheap*, *not wasteful*.

> It is more economic to buy in bulk.

should have *economical*.

Economic is the adjectival form of *economics*, the science of the production and distribution of wealth. The *economic state* of the country is its degree of financial prosperity. An *economic rent* is one necessary to cover costs.

An *economist*, however, may be either a thrifty person or a student of economics, usually the latter.

edible. See **inedible**.

effect. See **affect**.

effective

effective. See **efficient**.

efficient: producing an effect, in a competent way. An efficient man, machine, plan, etc., is one capable of working well. *Effective*: making an effect on something or somebody; *effective* defines success in applying work to a purpose or action.

The meanings are very close. To describe a police-force as *efficient* is to draw attention to its discipline, organisation and capacity for action; to describe it as *effective* is to draw attention to its success in doing what it has to do.

Efficient is not to be confused with *proficient*, meaning *skilful, expert*.

e.g. means *for example* (Latin: *exempli gratia*) and is used to introduce an illustration. It is normally preceded by a comma (or bracket), but a comma is normally not needed after it.

The expression should not be confused with i.e., which has a different function. See **i.e.**

ego is a term from psychology, meaning an individual's conscious personality, and it is both incorrect and unnecessary to use it as a substitute for *sense of self-importance*. Perhaps the error is from analogy with **egoism, egotism**.

egoism, egotism. The former has to do with selfishness, the latter with self-conceit and excessive use of *I*. The former is sometimes used when the latter is needed.

either or **either of** should be used of *two* persons or things, and be followed by a singular verb, in such cases as

Either proposal (*or* either of the proposals) (*of two referred to*) is feasible.

The plural verb is common and incorrect.

See **either ... or**.

either ... or 1. If *either ... or* (it is never correct to use *either ... nor*) is followed by a verb, the following rules should be observed.

(*a*) If the subjects are singular, the verb must be singular:

Either the architect or the builder *was* to blame.

The common error is to use the plural verb *were*. A little thought will show that the verb should be singular: either the architect *was* to blame or the builder *was*.

(*b*) If one of the subjects is plural (or both are) the verb should be plural:

Either the architect or the builders were to blame.

Either the architects or the builder were to blame.

(Some would argue that the verb should be governed by the

nearest noun, and that *was* is correct in the second of these sentences.)

(*c*) If pronouns are used, the nearer one governs the verb:

Either he or *I am* at fault.

is correct, though it is more elegant to say

Either he is at fault or I am.

Similarly

Either I or *he is* at fault.

Either she or *you are* at fault.

However, in the first of these sentences, courtesy suggests that *I* should be placed second:

Either he or I am at fault.

2. *Either ... or* should be placed carefully so that each half of the expression is a grammatically equivalent alternative:

Either open the window *or* the door.

is wrong because *open the window* and *the door* are not grammatically equivalent, the first being a sentence and the second a noun. Say

Open *either* the window *or* the door.

Similarly, not

They have gone *either* to Bradford *or* Leeds.

but

They have gone to *either* Bradford *or* Leeds.

or

They have gone *either* to Bradford *or* to Leeds.

so that what follows the *either* and the *or* are grammatically identical.

3. *Either* (like *neither*) may be pronounced with the first syllable rhyming either with *pie* or with *sea*, but the former is more common.

eke out: supplement; make something go further or last longer by adding to it.

The common error is to use *eke out* as if it meant simply *make to last longer* (as in *eke out the housekeeping money till the end of the month*) or *contrive to make* (a livelihood), as in

The peasants eke out their pitiful existence, knowing
that the central government is uninterested in their
plight.

The object of *eke out* must be something that is supplemented or added to:

More and more students are eking out inadequate grants
by taking part-time jobs.

elder, eldest

elder, eldest. As an adjective, *elder* means *senior of two people*, normally relations. *Eldest*: first-born or oldest surviving (usually of a family). It would therefore be correct for the mother of two sons to refer to one of them as *my eldest* or *my elder son*, though his younger brother should refer to him as *my elder brother*, not *my eldest brother*.

else, in *anybody else, everyone else, somebody else, who else*, etc., becomes *else's* in the possessive.
   See also **than**.

elsewhere. See **than**.

emotional and **emotive** are sometimes confused.
   Emotional: full of emotion (*an emotional reunion*) or liable to *feel* emotion (*an emotional person*).
   Emotive: likely or tending to *excite* emotion (*an emotive question; the emotive issue of capital punishment*).

enable means *make able*, not *make possible*.

energise means *infuse energy into* (a person, work). It should not be confused with **enervate**.

enervate: weaken, usually physically or mentally. It is often wrongly used as if it meant *stimulate* or *invigorate*.
   The atmosphere at the conference was wonderfully
   enervating.
is incorrect. The atmosphere could have been enervating, but it could not have been wonderfully enervating. See **energise**.

enough. See **tautology**.

enquire, enquiry are correct, as are **inquire, inquiry**. It is now common for *enquire* and *enquiry* to refer to the asking of a question, and *inquire, inquiry* to the making of an investigation. Thus *enquire* = ask, *inquire* = investigate.

ensure means *make certain*, and should not be confused with *insure* which means *secure the payment of a sum of money in event of loss of or damage to property or life, by paying a premium*.

envisage: set before the mind's eye. The word is best used in this sense of visualising something, and not as a loose alternative to *think, expect*, etc.

equal to, not *equal for* (in such expressions as *It was a hard climb, but they were equal to it*), nor *equal with* (in the sense of *They wish their wages to be equal to those of other skilled workers*).

50

equally as is wrong. Use one word or the other but not both, because they have identical functions. Thus either

> The return match was equally memorable.

or

> The return match was as memorable.

but not

> The return match was equally as memorable.

which is an example of **tautology**.

Likewise

> Gas is equally (as) expensive as electricity.

should be either

> Gas is as expensive as electricity.

or

> Gas and electricity are equally expensive.

Just as one says

> This concerns Britain and France equally.

one must say

> This applies equally to Britain and (*not* as) to France.

errata is the plural of *erratum*.

escalate and **escalation** are in vogue. They express nothing not already available in *grow* and *growth* except the pretentiousness of those who prefer them.

Esq. (abbreviation of Esquire) is sometimes used when addressing a letter to a man: *Henry Fisher, Esq.*, never *Mr Henry Fisher, Esq.* The custom, thought to lend dignity to the addressee, is dying.

etc. is the abbreviation of the Latin *et cetera*, meaning *and other things*. That being so, it should not be applied to people.

It is wrong to write *and etc.*, or to say *and et cetera*, because the *et* already means *and*.

Etceteras may be used as a single word meaning *extras* or *sundries*.

If *etc.* concludes a sentence, it should be followed by a second full stop, though some writers and typists, and all printers, prefer only one.

ethnic. See **racial**.

euphemism is the use of a pleasant form of words to describe something less pleasant, or to avoid direct statement. An advertisement which insists that a certain credit-card 'says more about you than cash ever can' means 'It is more fashionable to be in debt than to pay cash on the nail.' Other examples: *cosmetic deficiency* (ugliness); *gay* (homosexual); *make love* (have sexual intercourse); *put to sleep* (kill).

euphoria (adjective *euphoric*) means *state or feeling of well-being*, and

even

should not be used to mean *optimism, hopefulness* or *confidence*, as it often is by those who prefer an uncommon or fashionable word they do not understand to a common word they do.

even must be carefully placed. It is used to invite comparison between something which is named or stated, and something which might have been. The placing of *even* indicates the precise point of comparison:

Even he (of all people!) *didn't reply to the invitation.*
He didn't even reply to (much less accept) *the invitation.*
He didn't reply even to the invitation (quite apart from other communications he has been sent).

event. The expression *in the event of* is legitimate, though it is seldom superior to the more concise *if*.

If *in the event of* is followed by a verbal noun, as in

In the event of their *arriving* late ...

note that *their* is correct, not *them*, for exactly the same reason that *their* is needed in

In the event of their late arrival ...

See **verb 5 (c).**

eventuate, like many Americanisms, merely expresses in four syllables what perfectly adequate older words (*happen, result*) express in fewer.

ever is sometimes added to the interrogatives *who? how? when? what?* etc., to add emphasis. In such cases, it should be written as a separate word:

What ever made him do it? (i.e. What on earth ...)
When ever did I promise that?
How ever did you manage?
Where ever have you been? (i.e. Where in the world ...)
Who ever heard of such a thing?

just as one would automatically write

Why ever did he come?

with *why* and *ever* as two separate words. Compare

He's out *whenever* I call. (i.e. on whatever occasion)
Whoever said that was mistaken.
Do *whatever* you wish.

Here, *ever* is not added as a separate word for emphasis: it is part of the words *whatever, whoever,* etc.

See also the entry under **never**, which applies equally to *ever*.

every needs a singular verb:

Every police force in the six counties *has* been alerted.

See **everyone.**

52

everybody means *every person* and is singular.

> Everybody made up their own minds.

is incorrect for

> Everybody made up *his* own mind.

Similar errors occur when other singular words (*anyone, anybody, no-one, nobody, everyone, somebody, someone*) are followed by plural pronouns instead of the singular *he, himself, him, his* (which do duty for both sexes).

If *everybody, anyone, anybody*, etc., is the subject of a verb, the verb must be in the singular too:

> Everybody in the town *is* opposed to the proposal.

everyone (one word) means *all the people* and is singular. It is therefore correct to say

> Everyone enjoyed *himself*. (singular)

not

> Everyone enjoyed *themselves*. (plural)

Himself does duty for *himself or herself*.

Every one (two words) is used of things, as in

> Every one of the bottles was broken.

These meanings of *everyone* and *every one* should be clearly distinguished.

See **everybody**.

evince is sometimes used as if it meant *cause to show*:

> The publicity campaign evinced little interest.

(i.e. the campaign did not stimulate people to show much interest).

This is incorrect. *Evince* means *show*:

> The public evinced little interest.

exceedingly, excessively. The former means *very great, very much*: the latter means *too great, too much*. The adjectives *exceeding* and *excessive* are similarly differentiated.

exceptionable: open to exception or objection. The opposite is *unexceptionable*, meaning *perfectly satisfactory*.

These words should not be confused with *exceptional* (forming an exception; unusual) and *unexceptional*. There is sometimes confusion between *unexceptionable* and *unexceptional*. The correct meanings are illustrated in

> The child's behaviour was *unexceptionable* (i.e.
> satisfactory: one could not take exception to it).
> The child's behaviour was *unexceptional* (i.e. as one
> would expect: there was nothing exceptional about it).

exclamation mark. The exclamation mark (!) should be used sparingly, and not to indicate merely mild surprise, sarcasm or amusement. See **interjection** for the correct use.

excuse. Although *Excuse me* is a correct form of apology, such usage as

> Excuse me arriving late.

or

> Excuse me not arriving earlier.

is wrong, because *arriving* in both examples is a noun-equivalent, object of the verb *Excuse*, requiring the adjectival *my*, not *me*, exactly as one would say

> Excuse *my* late arrival.

See **verb 5 (c)**.

expedient, **expedience**, **expediency** are sometimes used interchangeably, but their precise meanings should be noted:

expedient (adjective):	advantageous, fit, proper, suitable.
(noun):	device, contrivance.
expedience (noun):	speed of execution; dispatch.
expediency (noun):	quality of being expedient; consideration of what is advantageous or politic (as distinct from what is just or right).

explanation of, not *explanation for*.

explicit: stated in detail; definite; (of persons) outspoken. *Implicit*: not expressly asserted, but insinuated, hinted, implied, indirectly expressed. An *explicit meaning* is plainly stated; an *implicit meaning* is intended and understandable, but not directly expressing all that is meant.

Implicit has the additional sense of *unquestioning, absolute*, as in *implicit trust, implicit faith*.

See also **infer**.

explore every avenue is a prominent example of **cliché**, and has the additional disadvantage of making poor sense, since exploration normally takes place in more challenging territory than an avenue.

exquisite is pronounced with the accent on the first syllable, not the second.

extent. For *to a greater or less extent* see **lesser**.

extrapolate: calculate from known terms a series of other terms which lie outside the range of the known terms. This is a precise and useful word, and there is no justification for using it as a high-sounding substitute for *calculate, deduce,* or even *guess.*

F

face up to. 'A needless expression, the result of the tendency to add false props to words that can stand by themselves' (Partridge). *Face* is sufficient.

facile always has derogatory overtones. A *facile argument* is fluent but superficial, even foolish.

fact. See **in actual fact.**

fact that. The expression *the fact that* is useful, but its overpopularity is illustrated in the following, from a letter written by two student union officials to a newspaper:

> In view of the fact that our prisons are overcrowded, and indeed contain many prisoners who need not be there, and also taking into consideration the fact that the Government ...

The opening six words could be replaced by one (*since, as*), as could the seven words in the second italicised phrase. Such economy would have been particularly welcome in a lengthy sentence of which only the first third is quoted.

fantastic means *extravagantly fanciful, capricious, eccentric*; *grotesque or quaint in design.* As an all-purpose adjective or exclamation expressing pleasure or approval it is over-used and misused.

farther, further are both comparatives of *far*, the superlatives being *farthest* and *furthest* respectively (see **adjective 1, 2**). Both forms may be used when referring to distance, but *further, furthest* are used when referring to time (*until further notice*) or extent (*further enquiries*).

Only *further* may be used as a verb, meaning *help on, promote, favour*, as in *to further one's plans.*

fascinate. One is fascinated *by* a person or *with* a thing (Partridge). See **fascination.**

fascination: irresistible attraction. It is therefore correct to say

> Horses have a fascination for her.

but not

> She has a fascination for horses.

unless the intended sense is

Horses are fascinated by her.

The correct formula is *fascination for* + person.

See **fascinate**.

feasible. It would be a pity if this word were to oust *possible* and *probable* from the language. There are occasions when *feasible* (capable of being done) is necessary, but there are also occasions when it is used unnecessarily instead of *possible*, *probable*, etc.

few is the opposite of *many* (*a man of few words*). *A few* is the opposite of *none* (*He agreed to say a few words*). In other words, *few* = some and not many; *a few* = some and not none (Fowler). See **comparatively**.

fewer. See **less**.

fictional is the adjective from *fiction*: a fictional character is one existing in literature. *Fictitious* = not genuine: a criminal, escaping from justice by a fictitious story, may flee to another country where he assumes a fictitious name.

figurative. See **metaphor**.

fill out, as in *to fill out a form*, is unnecessary: *fill in* and *fill up* are more accurate. *Fill out* means *enlarge to the desired limit*

The sails filled out as the wind strengthened.

or *become rounded in outline*

His face has filled out since his illness.

final should not be used before such words as *completion*, *ending* or *upshot*, the definitions of which already include the notion of finality. See **tautology**.

finalise is a disagreeable new word, probably here to stay, but worth avoiding in favour of *finish*, *complete* or *conclude*.

fine-tooth comb. The over-used expression *To go through something with a fine-tooth comb* means to go through it meticulously as if using a comb with fine (i.e. very thin and closely set) teeth. To misplace the **hyphen** (*fine tooth-comb*) or to pronounce the expression with the stress on *tooth* changes the sense to 'an attractive comb with teeth' or even 'for teeth', which are respectively tautological and nonsensical.

finite verb. See **verb 3**.

first. The old idea that one must use *first* (never *firstly*), then *secondly*, *thirdly*, etc., to begin sentences or paragraphs that list points, is now usually regarded as nonsensical. Either *first* or *firstly* is correct, and *firstly* is by far the more common.

See also **former**.

first person. See **person**.

first two. It is normal to say *the first two* rather than *the two first*. See also **first**.

firstly. See **first**.

flagrant does not mean the same as **blatant**.

focus may become *focused* or *focussed*, *focusing* or *focussing*. The *-ss-* form is the more common.

folk. The plural *folks* is normally reserved for members of one's family. Otherwise use *folk* as a plural noun (*The folk next door, folk-songs*).

following is sometimes used instead of *after* with ludicrous effect, as in this quotation from a newspaper report on an air-show:

Following the fly-past came the refreshments.

The unnecessary use of *following* instead of *as a result of* or *because of* can produce similar looseness.

forecast has the past tense and past participle *forecast* or *forecasted*, but the latter is so unusual as to sound wrong.

former. The expression *the former* (with or without a following noun) can only be used when *two* persons or things are being referred to. The following is incorrect:

Cinema, television and theatre, the former of which
offers actors the most substantial financial rewards ...

Instead of *former* use *first* or *first-mentioned* when more than two items are being referred to. See **latter**.

formidable is pronounced with the accent on the first syllable, not the second.

formula may have the plural form *formulae* (pronounced *-ee*) or the more English *formulas*.

fresh fields. See **woods**.

fulfil is so spelt. The past tense is *fulfilled*.

full stop. Used to mark the end of a **sentence** or to denote **abbreviation**.

further. See **farther**.

future

future. See **near future**.

future tense. See **verb 2**.

G

gaffe means *blunder* and should not be confused with *gaff*, a word which has several meanings and which most commonly occurs in the slang expression *blow the gaff*, meaning *divulge a secret*.

genitive. A noun or pronoun is said to be *in the genitive case* if it is expressing possession:

Spain's exports; *your* good fortune.

In this Dictionary, the term *possessive* is preferred. See **possessive, pronoun**.

genius has two plural forms, which must be distinguished: *geniuses* (persons of genius) and *genii* (guardian spirits). The latter is also the plural of *genie*, a sprite or goblin in Arabian tales.

See also **journalese**.

gerund. See **verb 5 (c)** and **participle**.

get. A multi-purpose word, especially with prepositions: get up, get on, get in, get back, get off, get out, get to, etc. Frequent use of this verb is to be avoided in the interests of variety and interesting style; alternative words are usually available.

golf. The pronunciations *gof* and *gohf* are now regarded as pretentious.

goodness' sake, for. Note the irregular punctuation *goodness'*. See **possessive 4**.

got. See **get**.

gourmand, like *gourmet*, means connoisseur of good food, but has overtones of gluttony which *gourmet* lacks.

graffiti is plural; the singular is *graffito*, meaning writing or drawing on a wall. *Graffito* is, however, hardly ever used, and *graffiti* as a singular word is now common.

gram, gramme. Either spelling is acceptable, but the former is becoming the more common, as it is in *milligram*, etc.

grammar is frequently mis-spelt, as it is in the following (from an advertisement for a system of language tuition!):

> One hundred years ago, Maximilian D. Berlitz observed people struggling through grammer books ...

greater. See lesser.

grievous is an adjective formed from *grieve*, and should not be mis-spelt or mispronounced *grievious*.

guerrilla (or *guerilla*) is a quite different word from *gorilla* and is pronounced differently, with a distinct *ger* as the first syllable. It comes from a Spanish word meaning *little war*.

guess. The American expression *I guess (so)*, meaning *I think (so)* or *I feel sure*, is worth resisting on the grounds that, in English, *guess* has a distinct meaning (*estimate, conjecture*) which there is no point in blurring by using it to mean something else. *I think* and *I feel sure* are both short and precise; *I guess* should only be used to mean *I guess*, not *I think*.

guide-lines. One normally thinks of a guide as somebody or something helpful, pointing the way but to be ignored if one chooses. But *guide-lines* is now used to mean *directing principles* as often as it is used to mean *guiding principles*. Politicians have been largely responsible for this confusion, because 'guidance' sounds more palatable than 'direction'. People who value honesty in language use *guide-lines* to mean *guiding principles*. If *direction* or *directing principles* are intended, say so.

H

h is pronounced *aitch*, not *haitch*. See **a** and **hotel**.

hair-brained. See **hare-brained**.

handful: small number; quantity that fills the hand. The plural is *handfuls*, despite a quite common belief that the educated usage is *handsful*. A *hand full* is a hand full of something; the plural is *hands full* (as in the expression *to have one's hands full*, i.e. to be very occupied). Also *basketful, basket full; bucketful, bucket full*.

hanged is used of capital punishment, including such expressions as *I'll be hanged if I'll do it* (I most certainly will not do it) and *Well, I'm*

harass

hanged (expression of surprise). In all other cases, *hung* is the correct past tense and past participle of *hang* (e.g. when speaking of pictures being *hung*).

harass has the accent on the first syllable, and the American pronunciation (with the accent on the second) is to be avoided. Exactly the same is true of the noun *harassment*.

hare-brained. It is a widespread belief that rash persons have brains made of hair. The correct expression is *hare-brained*, which can be applied to madcap schemes and ideas as well as to people. Whether or not the hare deserves this stigma is immaterial.

hardly is virtually a negative:
> He *hardly* ever comes.

means
> He almost *never comes*.

Care should be taken not to add a second negative illogically:
> He never, or hardly never, was seen in public.

should have *hardly ever*, because *hardly never* is the opposite of what is intended.

See **double negative**.

hardly ... when is correct (never *hardly ... than*) in such cases as
> The building was hardly finished *when* the first cracks appeared.

have got. The *got* is frequently unnecessary and should be omitted as often as possible.

hedonism, the doctrine that pleasure is the chief good, is pronounced *hee-*, as are *hedonist*, etc.

heinous. The first syllable rhymes with *pain*, not *keen*.

help but, as in *You can't help but admire his courage*, is wrong. *Help*, in the sense *refrain from*, requires the gerund (*You can't help admiring his courage*). *But*, in the sense *otherwise than*, is correct in such contexts as *You have no choice but to do it*, but is incorrect after *help*.

For an explanation of *gerund*, see **verb 5 (c)**.

hero has the plural *heroes*.

hers is never spelt *her's*. See **pronoun 3 (a)**.

hesitancy, hesitation. The former is the *quality* of hesitation, i.e. indecision. The latter is the *action* of hesitating.

historic: noted in history; memorable; famous. *Historical*: of history, having to do with the historian or the past (*of historical interest, a historical novel*). But *a historic victory, a historic meeting*.
See **hotel**.

history. See **hotel**, **tautology**.

hoi polloi is Greek for *the many* and has come to be superciliously applied to *the common herd, the uneducated masses* or *the rabble*, though sometimes light-heartedly. If one wishes to give the impression that one has had the benefit of a Classical education, one says simply *hoi polloi*, never *the hoi polloi*, because *the* and *hoi* mean the same thing.

homo- is a prefix indicating sameness. Thus *homogeneous* (of the same kind), *homosexual* (having a sexual propensity for one of the same sex), etc. The first syllable rhymes with *bomb*, not *home*.

honorary is spelt so. It is usually found in such expressions as *honorary secretary, honorary treasurer*, where it means *unpaid*. It is sometimes confused with *honourable* (worthy of respect).

honoured. The expression *more honoured in the breach than the observance* does not mean *more often broken than kept* but *better broken than kept*. Hamlet first used the words, referring to a custom that it was more honourable to break than to observe; the quotation is often mis-used.

hoof may have either *hoofs* or *hooves* as the plural. The former is the more usual. See also **roof**.

hopefully means *full of hope*. It does not mean *I hope* or *it is hoped*. The rules are simple:
1. *Hopefully* means *full of hope*.
2. Only people can be full of hope. Thus, uses such as *Hopefully, the stain will not show* are illiterate.
3. *Hopefully* is an adverb, and must be correctly applied to a verb. *The climbers set off hopefully* is correct. *Hopefully, all the terrorists are now dead* is not correct, unless the intended sense is that they are dead in a condition of hopefulness.
　　The word is used correctly in *To travel hopefully is a better thing than to arrive*. The increasingly common habit of using it in such contexts as *Hopefully, the weather will remain fine* is absurd, because the weather is incapable of remaining fine while full of hope. Such use is also unnecessary, given the availability of simple and correct alternatives (*I hope* or *It is to be hoped that the weather will remain fine*).
　　Like many Americanisms, however, this wrong use of *hopefully*

is now so widespread that it will probably become standard English in due course. The reader is urged to resist this growth, and to use *hopefully* only when it means *full of hope*.

hospitalise. See **containerise**.

hostile should be followed by *to* or *towards*, not by *against, for*, etc.

hotel. It is still considered correct not to sound the *h*, but the resultant *an hotel* is rather old-fashioned. It is certainly acceptable, and indeed more common, to sound the *h* and say *a hotel*.

It used to be considered proper to refer to *an* historian or *an* historical novel (the *h* being either sounded or silent), but this custom has now given way to the pronunciation *a* historian, *a* historical novel, with a sounded *h*.

how is sometimes used ambiguously, as in *I told him how I'd waited for two hours*. If the intended sense is *in what manner or fashion I had spent the time waiting*, the sentence is correct; it is more likely, however, that *how* is intended to mean simply *that*, in which case *that* should have been used.

How is sometimes used wrongly instead of *what*. Such common expressions as *Do you see how I mean?* should have *what* instead of *how* when the intended sense is *what*.

however. See **but ... however, comma 7** and **ever**.

humour, humorous. Note the spellings. The latter is commonly mis-spelt *humourous*. Note also *humorist* and *good-humoured*.

hyper- is a prefix meaning *over, above, exceeding, excessive*. *Hypercritical* (very critical) should not be confused with *hypocritical* (simulating goodness).

hyphen. Used to join two (occasionally more than two) words into a single, compound word: flower-seller, sharp-edged, life-sized, British-made goods, twin-engined, Anglo-American, mother-in-law.

Prefixes such as *non, ultra, multi, co, pre, anti* often take hyphens (non-stick, ultra-cautious, multi-national, co-founder, pre-school, anti-freeze) though many such words follow a common pattern of dropping the hyphen when they are taken into common use (coeducation, hypermarket, cooperation). See **prefix**.

The addition of prepositions or adverbs to words to form compound nouns requires the use of a hyphen: lay-by, let-out, stand-in, go-ahead, after-effects.

Numbers from twenty-one to ninety-nine (excluding single words) require hyphens, as do other compounds using numbers: six-footer, four-seater, seven-berth.

The omission or careless use of hyphens can cause confusion: there is a difference between *twenty three-ton lorries* and *twenty-three-ton lorries, re-cover* and *recover, loud-speaker* and *loud speaker, 200-odd pages* and *200 odd pages, co-respondent* and *correspondent.* The *Sunday Times* recently referred to a man with nine inch-long feet, and an advertisement once claimed, 'Our strings are used by a cross section of the Hallé Orchestra.' Near the Museum of London is an illiterate roadsign reading CAR SET DOWNPOINT.

Because hyphened words often, in the course of time, drop the hyphen and are spelt as one word, it is wise to consult a dictionary if there is doubt about the spelling. If a dictionary is not handy, insert the hyphen: over-caution is preferable to ambiguity. But make sure that the appropriate words are hyphenated: a superfluous hair-remover is a hair-remover that is not wanted.

The hyphen must be distinguished from the **dash**.

hyphenate, meaning *join with a hyphen*, is unnecessarily long, because *hyphen* exists as a verb. Although *hyphenated words* is correct, *hyphened words* is better.

hypothesis has the plural *hypotheses* (pronounced *-ees*).

I

I. Courtesy demands that *I* (or *me*) is placed last in such combinations as *My colleagues and I, for you and me*, etc.

identical with, not *identical to*.

idiom: the forms of expression which are peculiar to a language, in that they often evade the normal rules of grammar and have meanings or implications unconnected with the normal meaning of the words used: for example, the idiomatic uses of *turn* include *do it by turns* or *turn and turn about* or *in turn*; the idiomatic phrase *to warm the cockles of one's heart* has nothing to do with the normal meaning of *cockle*.

i.e. means *that is to say* (Latin: *id est*) and introduces clarification, amplification or emphasis of what has already been expressed. It is usually preceded by a comma (or bracket), but a comma is normally not needed after it.

if

The expression should not be used to introduce an example. See **e.g.**

if 1. It is still regarded as correct to use *whether*, not *if*, to introduce a clause which

(*a*) is the object of a verb, e.g. after *know, understand, see*, etc. See **clause 2 (c)**;

(*b*) implies an alternative, e.g. *or not.*

Thus

When will you find out *whether* you've passed?

Ask the cashier *whether* he'll accept a cheque.

However, *if* would now be regarded as acceptable in such cases, though *whether* must be used if an alternative in the negative is stated:

The manufacturers must decide *whether or not* the project would be too costly.

2. *If* should be followed by *were* (instead of *was*) in clauses which express a hypothesis that is not a fact:

If I (*or* he, she, it) *were* to arrive next Thursday, would that be convenient?

if and when is a common expression which is invariably wrong, either *if* or *when* being perfectly adequate by itself.

ignoramus, meaning *ignorant person*, has the plural *ignoramuses*.

ilk does not mean *kind* or *sort*, as in

Highly paid tennis players, and others of that ilk, are destroying traditional sportsmanship.

The word occurs only in Scots family titles.

illegible. There is a useful distinction between *illegible* (not legible, indecipherable) and *unreadable* (too boring, difficult, etc., to read).

image is now well established as an alternative to *reputation* or *impression made*, and as a substitute for the older *idea* or *picture*. An image is something fabricated, and it is an interesting comment on society that one should hear so much of the *image* of politicians or the *brand-image* of manufactured goods. Those who use the word in such senses should consider the difference between image and reality.

imaginary: existing only in the imagination. *Imaginative*: using the imagination, having a powerful imagination. An imaginative plan is one that shows the planner's powers of imagination; an imaginary plan exists only *in* someone's imagination.

imbue is often ignored in favour of incorrect uses of **instil** and **infuse**. It means *inspire* (with feelings) and can, unlike *instil* and *infuse*, be applied to people:

> He has the ability, essential to good managers, of
> imbuing his colleagues with a determination to succeed.

immoral, meaning *opposed to morality, morally evil*, should not be confused with *amoral*, meaning *unconcerned with morals*, nor with *immortal*, meaning *undying*.

imperative. See **mood**.

imperfect tense. See **verb 2**.

implement is spelt so, both as noun and verb. As a verb, it is over-used and, as Gowers says, 'the occasional use of *carry out*, *keep* or *fulfil* for a change would be refreshing'.

implicit. See **explicit**.

imply. See **infer**.

impracticable: incapable of being put into practice; unmanageable:

> The plan, though sound in theory, is impracticable.

Impractical (the opposite of *practical*): incapable of putting into practice. An impractical person is one who is poor at doing things.

impractical. See **impracticable**.

in actual fact may once have had some slight merit as an emphatic version of *in fact*, but such emphasis has been lost through over-use of the expression, which now means no more than the shorter and preferable *in fact*.

in between is an example of **tautology**: *between* is sufficient.

in connexion with is seldom preferable to the more concise *about*, and is a rather vague, multi-purpose expression for which a more precise alternative can usually be found.

in depth, a fashionable cliché, is an adjectival expression (an *in-depth survey* or *a survey in depth*) we can well do without. It means no more than *detailed*.

in-law. One may refer colloquially to one's *in-laws* (usually the parents or brothers and sisters of one's husband or wife), but the formal plurals are *mothers-in-law*, *daughters-in-law*, etc.

in lieu of. See **lieu**.

in order that should be followed by *may* or *might,* as in
> In order that no misunderstanding may arise ...
The same applies to *that* when it means *in order that.* See **may 3**.

in respect of, not *in respect to.*

inapplicable is pronounced with the stress on the second syllable, not the third.

incomparable is pronounced with the stress on the second syllable, not the third.

incredible: impossible or hard to believe. *Incredulous* (applied only to people) = not believing, i.e. showing incredulity.

incredulous. See **incredible**.

inculcate: urge, impress (fact, habit, idea) persistently (*upon* or *in* a person, person's mind, etc.). Thus a school may *inculcate good habits of learning in its pupils.* It may not have *pupils who are inculcated with good habits of learning* (though the pupils may be *imbued* with such habits). (See **imbue**.) Never use *inculcate with.*

indefinite article. See **a, an**.

index has the plural *indices,* but *indexes* is also correct and is increasingly found, except in mathematics and science.

indicative. See **mood**.

indict, meaning *accuse,* is pronounced so that *dict* rhymes with *sight.* The same is true of *indictment* (formal accusation, usually in a court of law).

indifferent is followed by *to*: *different* is followed by *from.*

indirect object. See **verb 4**.

indirect question. A direct question is the quotation of the actual words used when asking a question:
> What steps do you propose to take?
When a question is incorporated into a longer sentence, without quotation of the actual words used by the questioner, it is called an indirect question:
> I asked him *what steps he proposed to take.*
The italicised words are doing the work of a noun. In grammatical terms, the italicised words are the equivalent of a singular noun. Thus
> What steps he proposed to take *was* not clear.

indirect speech is the technical term used to describe the reporting of

66

what has been said or written, when the actual words said or written are not quoted exactly.

direct speech: Antony said, '*I come to bury Caesar.*'

indirect speech: Antony said *that he had come to bury Caesar.*

See **direct speech**.

indiscriminate, undiscriminating. The latter is usually applied to people, the former to aim, purpose, motive, impulse, selection, plan, method, treatment, behaviour (Partridge). An undiscriminating person is one who lacks discernment or acuteness in his judgments or tastes, etc. Indiscriminate buying likewise lacks careful consideration of distinctions between items.

industrial is the adjective formed from *industry* in the sense of trade or manufacture. Hence *industrial relations, industrial output. Industrious,* however, means *hard-working.*

industrious. See **industrial**.

inedible means *not to be eaten*, e.g. because dangerous: *uneatable* means *unpalatable, not fit to be eaten.* Beef is, of course, normally *edible*, but may be so tough as to be *uneatable*; if it goes rotten, it becomes *inedible.*

inevitably should be used with care. It is redundant if used with *must, have to* or other verbs which carry a sense of obligation needing no further reinforcement:

All *must inevitably* die.

says the same thing twice.

In other cases, *inevitably* should be used only if it adds meaning. Too often it is used automatically.

infectious. See **contagious**.

infer means *deduce* or *conclude* (something *from* something). The word is sometimes confused with *imply*, which means *express indirectly, insinuate, hint,* etc. The difference is neatly stated by Gowers: a writer or speaker implies what his reader or hearer infers.

What are you implying?

Am I to infer that ...?

inferior: lower (in rank, quality, etc.). Thus it is as ungrammatical to say *more inferior* as it is to say *more lower.*

inferior to, not *inferior than*. The following is incorrect:

English cars are inferior in quality and in appearance than imported ones.

inferiority complex. The word *complex* is, in this context, a technical term in psychiatry denoting a kind of mental abnormality set up by suppressed tendencies or experience (*C.O.D.*). Contrary to popular belief, it is usually marked by self-assertive rather than shy behaviour. A person may, however, feel inferior without suffering from a *complex* as defined. To say that such a person suffers from an inferiority complex, or that all shy people do, is therefore inexact or pretentious, or both. In the absence of 'mental abnormality' or 'suppressed tendencies', use *obsession with/conviction of one's inferiority*, or some such phrase, and leave *complex* to the psychiatrist.

infinite verb. See **verb 5**.

infinitive. See **verb 5 (a)**.

inflammable means *easily set on fire*. It must be differentiated from *inflammatory*, which means *tending to inflame* (usually with passion, and usually in a bad sense). Thus *inflammable substances*, an *inflammatory speech*.

inflexion. See **verb 2**.

inflict means *impose*. *Afflict* means *trouble*. Thus one may *inflict* punishment, or punishment may be *inflicted*. A person may be *afflicted* with misfortune, or misfortune may *afflict* him. An occasional error is to use *inflict* where *afflict* is needed. Only people are *afflicted*.

infuse. One cannot infuse a person. One can infuse something *into* a person. *Infuse* means *instil*.

    The historian who wrote

        He infused his soldiers with a sense of discipline.

meant either

        He infused a sense of discipline into his soldiers.

or

        He imbued his soldiers with a sense of discipline.

Imbue means *inspire* and is applied to people: one can imbue someone, or be imbued oneself. See **imbue**.

ingenuous, meaning *innocent, artless, open, frank*, should not be confused with *ingenious*, meaning *clever at contriving* or *cleverly contrived*. *Disingenuous*: having secret motives, not candid.

inhibition. In psychology, an *inhibition* is technically an instinctive or induced habitual shrinking from some impulse or action as a thing forbidden (*C.O.D.*). Like many useful psychological definitions, the word has been weakened by over-use into a pretentious and unnecessary alternative to *shyness* or *self-restraint*.

innocuous means *harmless*, which is not the same as *innocent*.

innovation. See **tautology**.

inpracticable and **inpractical** do not exist. See **impracticable**.

inquire, **inquiry**. See **enquire**.

inside of is incorrect for *inside* in such contexts as
> The repair will be finished inside of a week.
> You'll find it inside of the tool-box.
though such expressions are in common colloquial use.

There is, of course, no objection to *inside + of* when *inside* is a noun, as in
> The inside of the cupboard needs painting.

insinuate, in the sense of *hint*, usually means *hint in an unpleasant way*.

install and *installation*, but *instalment*. *Instal* is possible, but *install* is preferred.

instance is a word that is often used in wordy expressions when short ones may be available:
> in many instances   = frequently
> in a majority of instances = mostly
> in the first instance   = first(ly)

The word should be used sparingly. As is often true in English, the shorter expression is preferable to the long one.

Instance is often used as an alternative to *case*, and its over-use in such expressions as *in the instance of* and *in many instances* is open to the same objections as are made at **case 1**.

instil: put in by drops. Hence one can, metaphorically, instil ideas, feelings, etc., *into* a person; one does not *instil a child with* good sense, etc. See **infuse**, of which the same is true.
> It is a school that instils high standards.
is correct; so is
> It is a school that imbues its pupils with high standards.
but not
> It is a school that instils its children with high standards.

insure. See **ensure**.

integral is pronounced with the accent on the first syllable, i.e. as in *integrate*, not as in *integrity*.

integrate means *combine (parts) into a whole* and should not be used as if it meant the same as *join*, *coordinate* or *mix*.

intents and purposes. See **to all intents and purposes**.

interface is a piece of technological jargon denoting the areas of inter-
action between two different and independent systems, such as com-
puters and chemistry. Like many new words, it has been taken up
and broadcast by some who have only a hazy idea of its meaning,
so that the word has become a pretentious and unnecessary substitute
for *point of contact* or *common ground*, as in the newspaper article which
referred to the Liberal Party 'operating at the interface between
socialism and conservatism'. If the word cannot be used correctly, it
should not be used at all.

interjection. Usually a single word, often an exclamation or an expression of sudden feeling. Examples include
>Oh dear! Ah! Hurrah! Hello! Why? What? Right ho!
>What a pity! Sorry! Congratulations! Pardon?

They may be used as complete sentences (even though they usually
lack verbs); alternatively they may form part of sentences:
>Hallo, what's going on?
>Oh bother, I didn't realise that.

In such cases, interjections have no grammatical function: they should
be regarded as standing apart from the grammar of the rest of the
sentence.

The exclamation mark is optional and should be used only when
the exclamation or interjection is specially strong or noteworthy. Too
many exclamation marks produce a monotonously breathless effect.

into and **in to** have different meanings. Use *in to* when the sense of
these two words is separate, as when a tennis-player *runs in to the net*
or a footballer *throws in to a team-mate*. Use *into* when the senses are
inseparable, as when a car *runs into a wall* and converts it *into rubble*.
Of course, a tennis-player may run *into the net*, but that is not the
same as running *in to* it.

intractable. See **intransigent**.

intransigent is usually found as an adjective meaning *uncompromising*:
it is therefore applied to people. It should be distinguished from *intractable*, which is usually applied to things (e.g. to a problem or a difficulty) and means *not easy to deal with*; it can be applied to people, when
its meaning *stubborn* comes close to the sense of *intransigent*, but *intractable* always has the sense *unmanageable* or *rebellious*.

intransitive verb. See **verb 6**.

introspective and **introverted**. *Introspective*: looking into one's own thoughts and feelings. *Introverted*: with one's thoughts and feelings turned inwards upon themselves. In psychology, the terms have very precise meanings; in general usage, an introspective person is one who thinks about his own being and nature, while an introverted person (or introvert) is one who is very withdrawn.

invaluable is not the opposite of *valuable*. It means *of great value*, *priceless*. The opposite of *valuable* is *valueless* or *worthless*.

inverted commas. See **quotation marks**.

invitation. See **replies to invitations**.

invite as a noun, the abbreviation of *invitation*, is slangy, and should never be used in formal speech or writing.

involve is a popular word, often used as an easy substitute for a more precise one:

> How many people will be involved? (will take part?)
> Not very much cost will be involved. (entailed)
> The task has involved a lot of extra work. (necessitated)
> The power-failure did not involve any hospitals. (affect)
> The whole village will be involved in the celebrations.
> (will take part)

Sometimes *involved* can be omitted altogether:

> Fifteen thousand men are involved in the strike. (are on strike)

The word should be used only when a sense of complication (*an involved argument*) or entanglement (*involved in a legal dispute*) is needed. The same is true of *involvement*.

irony is saying the opposite of what is meant (e.g. saying *You're a bright one* to someone who has blundered). The tone of voice often indicates that the speaker has an ironical intention. See **dramatic irony**, **sarcasm**.

irreparable. See **repairable**.

-ise, ize. Because some English words end in -ise (e.g. *comprise, compromise, despise, devise, disguise, enterprise, exercise, improvise, supervise, surprise*), and others may be found in dictionaries ending in -ize (e.g. *civilize, criticize* (but *criticism*), *economize, organize, recognize, scandalize, standardize*), while others may have either ending (*summarise, temporise*), an attempt has been made to simplify matters by adopting -ise in all cases (except *prize*). Despite the protests of scholars, who argue that this is merely an easy solution to the problem of remembering which words must end in –ise and which words need not, the acceptance of –ise is now general, and is recommended as a means of avoiding error. When consulting dictionaries, remember that –ise words *must* be so spelt; all –ize words (except prize) may be spelt –ise.

–ise, **–isation**. See **containerise**.

iterate. See **reiterate**.

itinerary, not *itinery*.

it's and **its**. *It's* is an abbreviation of *it is*, the apostrophe denoting an omitted letter. *Its* is the possessive form of *it*, and means *of it*, in the same way that other possessive pronouns (e.g. *hers, yours, theirs*) are unusual in not having an apostrophe before the *s*. See **pronoun 3**.

it's me. See **pronoun 1 (b)**.

J

jargon is the technical vocabulary of scientists, technologists, computer experts and others who need, as a sort of short-hand, a private language peculiar to their profession. Jargon is not the same as **slang**, which has general currency. See **cant**.

Jargon is also the use of unnecessarily long words, unfamiliar terms or gibberish.

jobless. A word invented by journalists because *unemployed* takes up too much headline space. This is not a sufficient reason for admitting it into the language.

journalese is often used as a word expressing disapproval of a certain style of English. Not all journalese is bad: in fact the journalist's preference for simple words and short sentences is more to be admired than the use of ostentatiously long words and cumbersome sentences. Journalese is more usually defined, however, as the use of supposedly striking language to describe events to which it is inappropriate. It is a debasement of English when every surprise is a *shock*, every disagreement a *row* or a *split*, when every politician who criticises an opponent *lashes out, raps* or *blasts* him (note the popularity of the short word), and every control is a *crack-down* or *ban*. The habit extends to shops which *slash* prices by reducing them slightly, and to sports commentators who describe all skill as *genius*, excitement as *drama* and a missed goal as *tragedy*. The English language has shades of meaning which are too valuable to be blurred in this way, and language is devalued and cheapened when important words are applied to unimportant things.

Other overworked words which are in danger of losing their meaning through automatic use include *heavy* (as in *heavy losses*), *massive* (as in *massive reduction*), *crisis* (meaning difficulty) and *new* (in nine out of ten television advertisements).

See **jobless, push.**

judge, as a noun, is sometimes misused, as in the following, from a television commercial:

> I always think the best judge of character is how
> someone eats their ...

Judge should be *sign*. The *judge* is the speaker, not the manner of eating. (And *their* should, of course, be *his*, because *someone* is singular.)

judgement and **judgment** are both correct, but the latter spelling is the more common.

judicial means *connected with a court of law or legal process*, and should not be confused with *judicious*, which means *wise* or *sound in judgment*. A *judicial separation* is one legalised by a judge: a *judicious choice* is a sensible one.

just exactly, as in

> He arrived just exactly five minutes ago.

is an example of **tautology**. Use one word or the other, but not both together.

K

kerb. See **curb.**

kind. It is common to hear or read *these kind of* and *those kind of*, whereas correct grammar demands that the singular noun *kind* should have the singular adjective *this* or *that*, not the plural *these* or *those*. This usage is so common, and of so long a standing, that it is regarded as an acceptable colloquialism, but it is best avoided in favour of *this* or *that kind* and *these* or *those kinds*:

> That kind of people is not to be trusted.

or

> People of that kind are not to be trusted.

See **adjective 5, all kind of**.

kind of is often a meaningless addition to a sentence

> I kind of forgot it.

or as a substitute for *rather, to some extent*

> He's getting kind of forgetful.

Both of these uses are best avoided.

L

lamentable is pronounced with the emphasis on the first syllable, not the second.

large-size is beloved of advertisers (*large-size engine, large-size helpings*) and should be *large-sized*, though only advertisers know what is wrong with *large* on its own.

last can mean *most recent* as well as *final*, and must be used with care to avoid ambiguity.

last-named. See **latter**.

later on is merely a wordier version of *later*.

latter presents no problems when it is used to mean *belonging to the end of a period* (as in *the latter part of the financial year*), but when it is used, with or without a following noun, to mean *last* or *last-named*, it can only be applied to *two* persons or things, i.e. it means *second* or *second-mentioned*. The following is incorrect:

> Hughes, Smith and Callaghan played well, but the latter was injured shortly after half-time.

The latter should have been the *last-named*.

It is incorrect to use *last-named* when referring to only two: use *latter*. See **former**.

laudable, laudatory. The former means *praiseworthy*, the latter *praising*. A laudable speech is one that has merit; a laudatory speech is one in praise of someone or something.

lay and **lie** are often confused. *Lay* is normally transitive (*lay an egg, a wager, a trap, hands on, waste, open, claim, the table, it on thick,* etc.). The past tense is *laid*:

> The Headmaster laid down the law.
> The buyer has laid down certain conditions.

See **lie**.

leading question is often used as if it meant *difficult or pointed question*. It does not: it means a question which is so phrased as to prompt (*lead* to) the answer desired by the questioner (e.g. in a court of law, where it is not permitted).

learn. Both *learnt* and *learned* are correct. *Learn* is sometimes used illiterately instead of *teach*, as in

> My mother learned me never to tell lies.

least, like *less*, must be used of mass, volume, extent or quantity, not of number. Thus

> The candidate with the least votes will be eliminated
> after the first ballot.

is wrong: *least* should be either *fewest* or *smallest number of*. But

> He is the candidate with the least popularity.

is correct.

See **less**.

leave go (of) should be *let go (of)*.

leeway is the lateral drift of a ship to leeward (i.e. downwind) of her course. Such drift is undesirable! The term is used metaphorically, and correctly, in *to make up leeway* or *having leeway to make up* when the meaning has to do with recovery from an unwanted position or from undesirable circumstances. It is nonsense, however, to speak of *giving one (self) some leeway*, or *leaving/having some leeway*, as if *leeway* meant something good, such as a welcome breathing-space or room for manœuvre.

legitimise and **legitimatise** are unnecessary words, because they mean exactly the same as the older verb *legitimate*. However, both are now used to the virtual exclusion of *legitimate*. If the reader cannot bring himself to assist in the deserved revival of *legitimate*, let him at least prefer the shorter *legitimise* to the even more unnecessary *legitimatise*.

75

lenience, **leniency**. Both are possible; the latter is preferable.

less and **fewer**. Use *less* when referring to mass, volume, extent or quantity, and *fewer* when referring to numbers. Thus, *less choice* but *fewer choices*. The very common mistake is to use *less* as if it meant *not so many*, as in *less people*, which is wrong. As a useful general rule, use *less* with a singular noun and *fewer* with a plural one.

See also **degree** and **lesser**.

lesser is often misused in the common expression *to a greater or lesser extent*, where *lesser* should be *less*. *Greater* is the comparative form of *great* (*great – greater – greatest*), and should be balanced by the comparative form of *little*, which is *less* (*little – less – least*).

Lesser is the comparative form of *less* (i.e. a double comparative; there is no superlative) and means *not so great as the other or the rest*.

For an explanation of *comparative* and *superlative* see **adjective 1, 2, 3.**

See also **degree, less.**

lest is followed by *should*.

> He will have to choose his words very carefully, lest he should once again appear to be attempting to increase ill feeling.

This, however, is rather formal, and the present tense is normally found (*... lest he appears ...*).

The **subjunctive** is found after *lest*, as in *lest he be offended.*

let. See **rent.**

letter writing. In times past, grammar books and English lessons at school laid down complex rules about the ways in which letters should be begun and ended. Only two conventions are now used:

1. A formal letter, such as a business letter, addressed to a company or to a person whom the writer does not know, begins *Dear Sir,/ Dear Madam,/Dear Sirs*, and ends *Yours faithfully,* (not *Yours Faithfully,*) followed by signature. *Yours truly,* is also sometimes used today to close formal letters, and increasingly *Yours sincerely*. Note that there is a comma at the end of the *Dear Sir,* etc., and after *Yours faithfully, Yours truly*. The style of such letters will be formal and business-like, avoiding **colloquialism** or **slang.**

2. A less formal letter, sent to a named person who is not a friend, begins *Dear Mr/Mrs/Miss Smith*, and ends *Yours sincerely*. Each is followed by a comma. Full stops are not needed after *Mr* or *Mrs*, but note the use of commas. The style here will be more informal.

Letters between close friends are likely to begin and end with a wide range of endearments, and the style will be relaxed and conversational.

See **replies to invitations.**

liable to, followed by an infinitive, is often used when *apt to* would be better. *Apt to* means *having a* (usually unfortunate) *tendency to. Liable to* means *exposed to the risk of doing or suffering something undesirable.* The two definitions should be clearly differentiated. The safest rule is to prefer *apt to* unless a person (occasionally a thing) at risk of *suffering* is being referred to:

He is apt to fly into uncontrollable rages.

but

He is liable to be criticised.

liaison is sometimes mis-spelt.

libel and **libellous** refer to written or printed defamatory statements. See **slander.**

licence is the noun, *license* the verb (whence *licensee*). Though the two words are pronounced alike, as are *practice* (noun) and *practise* (verb), remember the difference by analogy with ad*vice* (noun) and ad*vise* (verb), where the spellings are in accordance with familiar rules of pronunciation, *advice* rhyming with *spice*, and *advise* with *disguise*.

lie, in the sense of *speak falsely*, presents few grammatical problems: the past is *lied*, and the present participle *lying*. But there are problems with *lie* in the general sense of *be at rest* or *reside, exist* (lie down, idle, in wait, heavy, low; the answer lies in increased output). It is often confused with *lay*. See **lay.** Note the following tenses:

I won't take it lying down.

When he saw how the land lay ...

The yacht has lain idle since the autumn.

(*Lie* in these senses is always intransitive, whereas *lay* is normally transitive.)

The tenses of *lie* in the sense *be at rest*, etc., are

Present	Present participle	Past	Past participle
lie	lying	lay	lain

The tenses of *lay*, however, are

lay	laying	laid	laid

lieu

The following, from the *Sunday Times*, illustrates the common confusion:

> After-dinner speakers will be pleased to know that he is laying low for a while.

lieu. In the unnecessary expression *in lieu (of)*, i.e. instead (of), in the place (of), *lieu* is pronounced *loo*.

lieutenant. Under the influence of American films and television series about the police, generations of British children are growing up in the belief that this word is pronounced *loo-tenant*. In English it is pronounced *lef-tenant* (though the Royal Navy prefers *le-tenant*).

lightning, as in *thunder and lightning*, should be differentiated from *lightening*, from *lighten* (make or grow lighter), as in *a lightening of the burden*.

likable is sometimes mis-spelt *likeable*.

like 1. The most common misuse of *like* is to use it as a **conjunction**. This is incorrect; use *as* instead. The following examples illustrate the *wrong* use:

> You should do like he does.
> This government is acting like the last one did.
> She sang like she had never sung before.

It is similarly incorrect to use *like* instead of *as if*; this often happens after *look* and *sound*:

> It looks (*or* sounds) like the exhaust pipe needs repairing.
> Things don't sound like they're going to improve.

See **conjunction**.

2. It is correct to use *like* as an adjective, meaning *similar to, resembling, characteristic of*:

> Have you ever seen anything like that?
> What does he look like?
> It was just like him to forget.

Note that *like* does not mean *identical to*. In

> He has promoted activities like motor-racing.

like should be *such as*.

3. *Like* is also a preposition meaning *in the manner of, to the same degree as*:

> He speaks French like a native.
> You should behave like him.
> Like many Americans, he is very friendly.

Note that if these sentences were slightly changed by the addition of verbs, *like* would then be used as a conjunction instead of a preposition, and would then be wrong (see **1** above):

He speaks French like a native does.

You should behave like he does.

Like many Americans are, he is very friendly.

In all three sentences, *like* must be replaced by *as*. See **conjunction** and **preposition**.

4. *Like* may be a noun (*his likes and dislikes*) and, of course, a verb.

5. Care must be taken to ensure that, when *like* is used, like things are compared. Consider the following (from the *Sunday Times*):

Like motherhood, we all believe in law and order.

The intended meaning is

We all believe in law and order as (instinctively as) we
believe in motherhood.

But by placing *Like motherhood* next to *we*, the writer produced a grammatical construction which means

We all, like (i.e. resembling) motherhood, believe in law
and order.

which is absurd.

Here are two other examples where *like* links, and therefore compares, two unlike things:

Like her husband, Queen Victoria's upbringing was
sheltered.

The two things which the writer intended to liken to each other are not *her husband* and *Queen Victoria's upbringing*, but either *her husband* and *Queen Victoria* or *her husband's upbringing* and *Queen Victoria's upbringing*. The correct versions are therefore

Like her husband, Queen Victoria had a sheltered
upbringing.

or

Queen Victoria's upbringing, like her husband's
(upbringing), was sheltered.

In these correct versions, *like* now links and therefore compares two like people or things.

Similarly, in

It is believed that this strike, like last year, could go on
for several weeks

the two things likened (i.e. linked by *like*) are *this strike* and *last year*. The intended comparison, of course, is between *this strike* and last year's strike, and so *last year* in the above sentence should read *last year's strike*. It will be noticed that, grammatically, the above sentence means that last year could go on for several weeks!

See also **not only ... but (also)** for another example of a similar rule.

lily. If the urge to quote Shakespeare is irresistible, it should be remembered that he wrote (in *King John*)

To gild refined gold, to *paint the lily* ...
Is wasteful and ridiculous excess.

See also **honoured**.

limited is overworked, and there are many synonyms: *small, little, scant, restricted, meagre, insufficient, inadequate,* etc. Particularly overworked are *a limited number of* and *a limited amount of*, which are wordy alternatives to *few* and *little*.

literally means *exactly in accordance with the meaning of the word(s)* to which *literally* is attached. To say that a thief was caught red-handed (i.e. in circumstances where his guilt was evident) is acceptable; to say that he was caught *literally red-handed* is acceptable only if he had red hands. *Literally* is often wrongly used in this way, merely as a means of emphasis, with some ridiculous consequences: *The players literally ran out of steam.*

See **metaphor**.

litigious (fond of going to law), not *litiginous*.

litotes is the technical name given to the device of expressing something by the negative of its opposite, e.g. *He is no fool* (= *He is clever*).

loan does not exist as a verb, except in America, and there is no good reason why it ever should, since *lend* exists and is adequate. There is no objection to *loan* as a noun, but avoid *He loaned me his car*, etc.

loath and **loth** (both of which mean *disinclined*) should not be confused with *loathe* (detest) despite the spellings of *loathing* (detestation) and *loathsome* (detestable). In *loath* and *loth* the *th* is pronounced as in *birth*; in *loathe* and *loathing* it is as in *these*; in *loathsome* it may be either.

look like. See **like 1**.

lose rhymes with *choose* but should not for that reason be mis-spelt *loose*, which means something quite different and rhymes with *juice*.

lose out (on). It needs to be asked whether *out* or *out on* add anything to the verb.

lots is singular unless it is followed by *of* and a plural noun or pronoun:
There *is* lots to see.
There *are* lots of places worth visiting.

low-budget, like *low-cost*, means *cheap*, a word too blunt for advertisers.

low-key is a curious cliché, because keys in music can be major or minor but never *low*. Those who wish to avoid the cliché have *unassertive* available.

low profile has become a cliché. To adopt a low profile is to be discreet and cautious, to refrain from making oneself a target. The origin of the metaphor is military: the lower the silhouette, the less the danger. In many cases, *to adopt a low profile* is a polite or pompous substitute for *to do nothing*.

luxuriant (growing profusely; exuberantly productive) should not be confused with *luxurious* (characterised by luxury). Thus a *luxuriant beard* and a *luxurious holiday*.

M

machination. The *ch* is pronounced *k*.

madam is so spelt in English, and the correct French spelling, *Madame*, is used only when writing to, or of, French ladies.

main clause. See **clause 1**.

maintenance is pronounced with the stress on the first syllable. The word is frequently mis-spelt, and mispronounced, as if its first two syllables were *maintain*.

major is overworked by newspapers, advertisers, etc., and should not be used to the exclusion of *large*, *important*, *big*, *momentous*, *main*, *prominent*, *chief*, *principal*, etc.
The primary meaning of *major* is *greater*, so *more major* is as ungrammatical as *more greater*.

majority means *greater number*; it should therefore be confined to numbers, and not used for mass, volume, quantity, etc., as it is in
The majority of the area has been affected by flooding.
Use *Most of* or *The greater/larger part of* in such circumstances.

malapropism

It is permissible to speak of *the great majority* meaning *almost all*, but it is quite wrong to say *the greater majority* (because it is mathematically impossible for any number to comprise two majorities, one greater and one less). Either *the great majority* or *the greater part*, but never *the greater* or *greatest majority*.

malapropism. Ludicrous misuse of a word, especially in mistake for one resembling it, as in Brendan Behan's *The Hostage* where the land-lady says, 'Men of good taste have complicated me on that carpet.' (The word derives from the character Mrs Malaprop in Sheridan's *The Rivals*.) Unintentional malapropism may also occur, as in
He's a veritable Casablanca.

mandatory has the stress on the first syllable.

many a ... should be followed by a singular verb:
Many a chess-player has ... (not *have*)

marginal and **marginally** are in danger of replacing *slight, small,* etc., and *barely, slightly, just,* etc., in accordance with the mistaken belief that the longer and slightly more unusual word is always preferable to the shorter and more familiar one. *Marginal(ly)* is acceptable in moderation, but not to the exclusion of other available words.

masochism is a form of perversion in which one derives pleasure from being hurt or humiliated. Not to be confused with **sadism**.

masterful: imperious, domineering. *Masterly*: very skilful. The former is often mistakenly used for the latter:
After lunch there was a masterful talk on flower-arranging.

masterly. See **masterful.**

materialise has a useful and special meaning: make material, represent as material; cause (spirit) to appear in bodily form; (of spirit) appear in bodily form. There is no good reason why the word should be used inaccurately, in place of readily available correct words, as it often is:
The strike did not materialise. (happen)
The expected crowds did not materialise. (arrive)
They made promises which did not materialise. (were never fulfilled)

mathematics is usually regarded as a singular noun.

maximise means *increase to the utmost*, and should not be used as a synonym for simply *increase*. It is an over-used word, and the writer

or speaker who finds himself using it frequently should ask himself
whether he is getting into a bad habit.

may has the past tense *might* and is used
    1. to express possibility:
        It may never happen.
        But for the weather, the expedition might have
        succeeded.
    2. to express permission:
        May we come in?
        He asked if he might keep it a little longer.
    3. after (*in order*) *that, so that, lest* (i.e. in adverbial clauses expressing
purpose, sometimes called *final clauses* – see **clause 2 (b)** for explanation):
        He is going to university so that he may become an
        engineer.
        He worked hard so that he might gain promotion.
Such uses are rather literary, however, and an infinitive is usually preferred:
        He is going to university *to become* an engineer.
    4. to express a wish:
        May you both be very happy.
        Long may she reign.
    5. in questions, to emphasise the uncertainty:
        Who may he be?
Might is also found colloquially in the present tense to suggest
action:
        On your way home, you might call at the
        post-office
or to complain of neglect of duty:
        You might help with the washing-up.
It similarly softens the tone:
        Might I say something?
is slightly gentler than
        May I say something?
See **can**.

maybe, meaning *perhaps*, must be differentiated from *may be*, the verb.
He may be ill, but *Maybe he is ill*.

meaningful is a quite useful new word, though it is currently over-
used, often adding nothing to the sense of an expression. In view of
its status as a near-cliché, it should be used sparingly, and only when
it adds meaning.

means, the plural of the noun *mean*, may be treated as a singular, as in *a means to an end*. In such cases, the rest of the construction should be adjusted accordingly:

> Is (*not* Are) there a means of getting there more quickly?

Means (as distinct from *a means*) can, of course, be followed by a plural verb:

> There *are* other means of transport.

media, in the sense of the *mass media of communication* (television, newspapers, etc.) is the plural of *medium* and should not be used as a singular noun, as it often is.

mediaeval and **medieval** are both correct spellings, the latter being now more common.

medicine is frequently mis-spelt *medecine*. Remember medical.

medium has the plural *mediums* when referring to spiritualism, and *media* in other cases.

medium-size should be *medium-sized*, and often simply *medium*.

meet up with is unnecessary for *meet*.

meet with is an Americanism which some people feel has a shade of meaning not present in *meet*; they say that *meet with* should be used of long meetings, and *meet* of casual ones. This is an unconvincing argument, and the two expressions are not in practice differentiated in this way, either in Britain or America. Besides, *confer with* is available to be used for a meeting that is not casual. Use *meet*, not *meet with*.

memorandum has the plural *memoranda*, but *memorandums* is correct and is increasingly found. *Memorandas*, however, is illiterate.

metaphor can be best understood by first examining *simile*, which is a comparison (using the words *as* or *like*) to explain, emphasise or decorate a statement:

> The newly appointed Foreign Secretary has taken to international diplomacy like a duck to water.

Other examples, which illustrate that popular similes are often close to **cliché,** are *white as a sheet, come down like a ton of bricks, keen as mustard, drink like a fish, bold as brass, safe as houses*.

Similes always state what the two things or persons being compared have in common. In the above list these 'points of comparison' are whiteness, coming down, keenness, drinking, boldness and safety. In

Earth stood hard as iron

the comparison is between *Earth* and *iron*, and the point of comparison is hardness.

Metaphor is also a comparison between two people or things that are usually unconnected, but *as* and *like* are not used, and the point of comparison is usually implied rather than stated. When Donalbain, in *Macbeth*, says

There's daggers in men's smiles

he means

There are threats of murder disguised by people's friendly behaviour, just as daggers may be hidden in innocent-looking clothing.

The last part of this (*just as daggers . . . clothing*) is a simile. All metaphors can be amplified in this way, to make explicit the point of comparison. All metaphors are, in fact, compressed similes. Note the much greater conciseness of

There's daggers in men's smiles,

the exercise of the reader's imagination in supplying the point of comparison himself, and the vividness of the juxtaposition of the near-opposite *daggers* and *smiles*.

Metaphorical language is not confined to literature. It is used very frequently in everyday English: mortgaged *up to the hilt*, come *unstuck*, a *flood* of complaints, a *ceiling* on wages, *ring the changes*, deny *point-blank*, *smell a rat*, sacred *cow*, *rock-bottom* prices, *spanner in the works*, *hot potato*, plan which has failed to *get off the ground*, change one's *tune*, *bend over backwards*. Individual words which are usually used metaphorically (i.e. not literally) include *windfall*, *concrete*, *framework*, *hallmark*, *turnover*, *saddle*, *corner-stone*, *elbow-room*, *back-pedal*, *yardstick* and very many others. When a dictionary defines a meaning as *figurative* (or *fig.*) it means *metaphorical*. For example, to *earmark* is, literally, to mark an animal's ear, usually a sheep's, as a sign of ownership; metaphorically, it means *assign to a definite purpose* as in *savings earmarked for our next holiday*.

While metaphorical language adds much vividness to English, metaphors can soon become jaded: see **blueprint**, **bottleneck**, **catalyst**, **hare-brained**, **leeway**, **target**. To resort to over-used metaphor is to risk colourless, second-hand English.

An occasional risk is the mixing of metaphors in an absurd way, as in the well-known

We have our backs to the wall: we must therefore put our shoulders to the wheel, our hands to the plough and our noses to the grindstone.

meter, as in *gas-meter*, etc., is not to be confused with *metre*, the unit of measurement (and of rhythm in poetry).

meticulous means *over-careful*; it originally meant *timid*, but this fact is not widely known, and the word is almost always used to mean *admirably careful of detail*. There are other words meaning this (*scrupulous, punctilious*, for example), and it is best to reserve *meticulous* for its special meaning of *over-careful*.

middle. See **centre.**

middle class should be written as two words when used as a noun, and hyphened when used as an adjective (*middle-class values*).

might. See **may.**

militate and **mitigate** are often confused because of the similarity of their sounds. Their meanings are quite different.
Militate = tell against a conclusion or result.
Expert evidence militates against the painting's authenticity.
means that the evidence calls the authenticity into question, or inclines to the conclusion that the painting is not authentic.
Mitigate = alleviate, soften, moderate (verb), lessen the severity of.
Prolonged rain will be needed to mitigate the effects of the drought.
The most common error is the use of *mitigate against* when *militate against* is intended. *Mitigate against* never makes sense.

minimise: reduce to, or estimate at, the smallest possible amount or degree.
The word does not mean *reduce, decrease, lessen*, etc., and is incorrectly used in such cases as
Wastage should be minimised to a certain extent.
because the final four words are meaningless when *minimised* means *reduced to the smallest possible extent*.
The idea of 'the *smallest possible* amount or degree' should always be present if *minimise* (or the ugly *minimisation*) is to be used.

minority. Like *majority, percentage* and *proportion*, this word tempts writers and speakers into unnecessary wordiness. *A small minority of* is seldom preferable to *few*.

minutiae means *precise or trivial details* and is plural.

mischievous has the stress on the first syllable, and there is no *i* after the *v*.

miss out (on). It is very doubtful if *out* or *out on* add anything to the meaning of the verb.

missile. In England, *missile* is not pronounced to rhyme with *whistle*, but with the final syllable rhyming with *file*.

mitigate. See **militate**.

mixed metaphor. Metaphor is a well-established and valuable literary device (see **metaphor**) but the insensitive use of metaphors in proximity with one another can produce a ludicrous mixture. Do not fall into the sort of error committed by the local politician who wrote to tell *The Times* that, at a recent event which had ended in a riot, the police had leaned over backwards to maintain a low profile!

moment in time, at this. A ghastly cliché. Use *at this time*, or *at this moment*, or simply *now*.

momentary, momentous. The former means *lasting only a moment*, the latter *of great importance*. Thus *a momentary pause* but *a momentous decision*.

Momentary is pronounced with the emphasis on the first syllable, not the second.

monosyllable: word of one syllable. See **syllable.**

mood. A verb may make a statement in a number of ways. These are called *moods*. There are four of them. They need not be memorised, but they are included because some grammar books refer to them. This book refers only to the first and the fourth, and only in the entry under **subjunctive**.

1. A verb which states a fact or asks a question is in the *indicative mood*:

A noise *was heard. Is* it raining?

2. A verb which states a command is in the *imperative mood*:

Come into the garden, Maud.

3. A verb which makes a statement in the most general way, without having a subject, is in the *infinite mood*:

To err is human.

See **verb 5 (a).**

4. For the *subjunctive* mood, see **subjunctive.**

moot is frequently pronounced as *mute* is. This is wrong. *Moot* is pronounced as written, and has quite different meanings from those of *mute* (see **mute**). *Moot* is most frequently found as an adjective (meaning *debatable*, as in *a moot point*) or a verb (meaning *raise for discussion*, as in *This policy was first mooted at last year's conference*).

morale

morale, with the final syllable pronounced *arl*, means *spirits, state of mind*, as in *the refugees' morale*, i.e. their confidence, happiness, discipline. It has nothing to do with *morals*, or *morality*.

more, most. The former is used in comparing two persons or things, the latter in comparing more than two:
> He is the more aggressive of the two players.
> He is the most talented player in the team.

more than one requires a singular verb, as in
> More than one famous statesman *has* been caught out in a similar way.

most should not be used in comparing two persons or things, as in
> The resort has two piers, of which the East Pier is the most visited.
Use *more* when comparing two things, and reserve *most* for comparison referring to more than two. See **adjective 1, 4, more, most**.

most, as an adverb, means *in the highest degree. Mostly*, also as an adverb, means *in the main*. There is therefore a substantial difference between *Lunch was most enjoyable* and *Lunch was mostly enjoyable*, but the difference was not noted by the journalist who wrote
> The Budget is designed to help those mostly in need.

mostly. See **most**.

Mr and **Mrs** do not need full stops after them.

Ms, apparently pronounced either *Miz* or to rhyme with the second syllable of *farmers*, is preferred to *Mrs* or *Miss* by liberated women who do not regard their marital status as a fit subject for public knowledge. Mercifully, the use of *Ms* does not much exist outside a handful of newspapers which are written or read by liberated women. The word is foolish, ugly, meaningless and almost unpronounceable, and deserves oblivion.

much less is often used where logic requires *much more*, as in
> It is difficult to reduce, much less to stamp out, the amount of tax evasion now being practised.
Expressed in full, this means
> It is difficult to reduce, and it is *much less* difficult to stamp out, the amount of tax evasion now being practised.
By rephrasing the sentence in full this way (i.e. by repeating the main

88

verb *it is difficult* where it was previously 'understood' in the *much less* part of the sentence), it is made clear that the original wording expressed the opposite of what was intended. To decide between *much less* and *much more*, it is necessary to insert mentally the omitted main verb in this way. The following are correct uses of *much more* and *much less* (with the full versions of the sentences stated in brackets):

> He does not even permit it, much less approve of it.
> (He does not even permit it, much less *does he* approve of it.)
> It will be a long time before the building is even finished, much more brought into use.
> (... much more *will it be a long time before the building is* brought into use.)

must have, never *must of*, which is illiterate.

mute has to do with silence, as
>   1. an adjective, meaning *silent*.
>   2. a noun, meaning either a dumb person or an instrument for deadening the sound of some musical instruments.
>   3. a verb, meaning *deaden* (usually of musical instruments).

It is, with surprising frequency, confused with *moot*, which is pronounced differently. See **moot.**

mutual does not mean *common to two or more persons*. Such expressions as *our mutual friend* (i.e. a friend of me and you) and *a mutual acquaintance* (i.e. someone known to the speaker and another person) are incorrect English, though some would assert that usage has now sanctioned them. In

> Unemployment is the mutual enemy of government
> and the trade union movement.

mutual should be *common*.

Mutual is correctly applied to feelings, actions, etc., *felt, or done, by each to(wards) the other*, as in *mutual affection* (affection for each other), *mutual advantage* (advantage for both parties). It is safe to use *mutual* as a synonym for *reciprocal*.

Mutual is often used superfluously, and should have been omitted from the following, which can make their meaning plain without it:

> A mutual exchange of views.
> We have reached mutual agreement.

myself should not be used as a substitute for *I* or *me*, as it is in
> My colleagues and myself attended the funeral.
> It is convenient for both my wife and myself.

Myself should be used only in accordance with the rules given at **pronoun 4 (e)**.

N

near future. The common expression *in the near future* is unnecessarily long-winded, and *soon* is quite adequate.

nearly should be carefully placed.

> We nearly gave up (*i.e.* but we didn't give up).
> They gave up nearly everything (*i.e.* they did give up most of what they had).

need, as a verb, has some irregularities.

The normal third person singular is *needs*, as in

> This floor needs to be cleaned.

but in questions, or in the negative, *need* is normally used instead:

> Need it be cleaned?
> This floor need not be cleaned.

Note that the *to* of the infinitive (e.g. *to be cleaned*) is dropped when *need* is used instead of *needs*.

Need may also be used instead of *needed*:

> He came earlier than he need have done.

or

> He came earlier than he needed to have done.

negatives. *No*, *not* and *nobody* are negatives: so are *nothing*, *hardly*, *scarcely*, *neither*. Two negatives make a positive: thus

> I did not see nobody.

means

> I saw somebody.

See **double negative**.

It is a common error, especially with 'disguised' negatives such as *hardly* and *scarcely*, to use two negatives when only one is intended:

> I don't have scarcely any money. (*omit* don't)
> I didn't see hardly anything at all. (*change* didn't see *to* saw)
> He didn't go, and I didn't neither. (*change* neither *to* either)

negligent: careless; *negligible*: insignificant.

negotiate is sometimes mis-spelt.

neighbourhood. The expression *in the neighbourhood of* is sometimes unnecessarily wordy:

> The painting is expected to attract bids *in the neighbourhood of* half a million pounds.

Why not *of about*?

neither 1. The rules for *neither, neither of* and *neither ... nor* are the same as for *either*. See **either** and **either ... or**.
2. *Neither* must have a singular verb:

> Neither of the bills *is* accurate.
> Neither of us *knows*.
> ... the speeches, neither of which *was* ...

3. *Neither* is used of *two* persons or things. For more than two, use *none* or *not any*:

> Neither of the (two) shops was open.
> None of the (more than two) shops was open.

neither ... nor (never *neither ... or*). See **either ... or**, the rules for which are the same as for *neither ... nor*.

neologism: a newly coined word. See **containerise**.

never deserves careful placing.

> I never expected to find it.

means

> I expected never to find it.

i.e. the adverb *never* belongs to *to find* and should therefore be placed next to it. In other words, the finding, not the expecting, should be negatived.

news is regarded as a singular noun, as in *news travels fast*.

nice may mean *subtle*; *requiring precision, care, tact, or discrimination* as in *a nice dilemma/question/point/distinction*. Meaning *agreeable, attractive*, etc., it is one of the most over-used words in the language, and a more precise alternative should be found wherever possible.

ninth. Note the spelling.

no-one should be so written, though *no one* and *noone* are acceptable. Remember that *no-one* is singular, and follow the rules described under **nobody** and **everybody**.

no place meaning *anywhere* (*He couldn't find it no place*) is American and incorrect.

no sooner than often becomes distorted in use, as in
> No *sooner* had he finished the play, his first for seven
> years, *when* another was immediately commissioned.

Hardly ... when, scarcely ... when but *no sooner ... than.*

nobody means *no person* and is singular. Any associated verb or pronoun should be singular too.
> Nobody *is* allowed to do as *he* (not *they*) likes.
> Nobody *likes* to see *his* (not *their*) earnings lose their
> value.
> Nobody should fool *himself* about the likely outcome.

Note that *he, his, himself* do duty for both sexes.

See **everybody**.

nominative. A noun or pronoun is said to be *in the nominative* when it acts as the subject of a verb. See **pronoun** (especially **pronoun 1**), **verb 3**. Since only pronouns have different forms in the nominative and the accusative in English, the word *nominative* has little significance except with regard to pronouns.

non-finite verb. See **verb 5**.

none means *not any* and may be singular
> None of the milk *has* been delivered.

or plural
> None of the groceries *have* been delivered.

Some would argue that when *none* means *not one, no-one* or *no person*, the singular is better, but that when it means *no persons* the plural is correct. If this argument is accepted, the second example above should read *None of the groceries has been delivered.*

nor must be used if it is part of a *neither ... nor* construction, as in
> The guests found that *neither* the swimming pool, sun-
> terrace *nor* (not *or*) car-park had yet been built.

If a sentence contains *not* or *no* in the first part, it may matter little whether *nor* or *or* follows. In
> There was *no* swimming pool *or* sun-terrace.

it can be argued that *no* governs both the following nouns, and that it is therefore unnecessary to put a negative before *sun-terrace* to give extra emphasis to the complaint. But in
> In the past year, the company has suffered no strikes, or
> ever fallen behind in its delivery dates.

it is doubtful if the force of *no* can carry beyond the noun *strikes* to put the following verb also into the negative. The sense is that the company has *never*, not *ever* fallen behind; *or* should have been *nor*.

not. It is common to hear someone say

> I shouldn't be surprised if it didn't rain later today.

when he means

> I shouldn't be surprised if it *did* rain later today.

The mistake is surprisingly common in written English too.

not only ... but (also). A very frequent source of error. It is essential that the words which form the two parts of expressions introduced by *not only* and *but* (or *but also*) should be grammatically equivalent units (e.g. two nouns, two phrases, two clauses, etc.).

> *Not only* does the fall in the birth-rate vary from city to city *but also* from area to area within individual cities.

is wrong because *Not only* is followed by a sentence and *but also* by a phrase. Logic demands

> The fall in the birth-rate varies *not only* from city to city *but also* from area to area within individual cities.

or, more wordily,

> *Not only* does the fall in birth-rate vary from city to city *but (also)* it varies from area to area ...

In both these correct versions, notice that the words in both halves of the *not only ... but also* expressions match each other grammatically – two phrases in the first sentence, two sentences in the second.

Another illustration of wrong use:

> It is being argued *not only* that the Arts Council currently favours London too much *but* even intends to increase its subsidy.

To correct this, either place *not only* after *Council*, or add *that it* after *but*. The first correction produces the structure

> It is being argued that the Arts Council
> *not only* favours ...
> *but* intends ...

The second solution produces

> It is being argued
> *not only* that the Arts Council favours ...
> *but* that it intends ...

Both solutions now have *not only* and *but* followed by similar grammatical structures (verb plus object in the first, clause in the second). A simpler solution is to avoid *not only ... but also* in favour of *and*! For similar rules about grammatical equivalence, see **both ... and, either ... or 2, like 5**.

not so much as sometimes becomes ungrammatically distorted, as in

> He will be remembered *not so much* for the films he

made in the 1960s, when his popularity was fading, *but*
for those of the war years.
Here *but* should be *as*.

nothing is a singular word, and needs a singular verb.

Nothing except lies, excuses and evasions have been
heard since the rumours were first published.

should read *has been heard*. Grammar requires *nothing has*, not *nothing
have*. The verb *has* has been wrongly attracted into the plural by the
plural nouns *lies*, *excuses* and *evasions*. *Nothing* is, however, the subject
word.

noun. A noun is a word that names a person, place or thing.

1. A *proper noun* is a word naming someone or something unique,
such as a particular person or persons (Thomas Hardy, the Prime
Minister, Manchester United, the Hammond Sauce Works Band),
or a particular place (France, Everest, Thames, Fountains Abbey,
Dover, Duke Street, Langley Park School). Other proper nouns
include the days of the week, months of the year, other special
calendar names (Easter, August Bank Holiday, etc.) and names
given to animals (Fido), ships, houses, etc. Proper nouns always
begin with capital letters.

2. A *collective noun* is a word denoting a collection of people or
things (crew, audience, staff, herd).

A collective noun may be used with either a singular or a plural
verb, though it is best to use a singular one when the sense of the
sentence draws attention to the unity of the collection

The whole audience *is* now seated.

and a plural verb when a sense of disunity is indicated:

The flock *were* scattering in all directions.

See **pronoun 8 (b)**.

3. An *abstract noun* denotes, as its name suggests, a state, feeling or
quality (charity, education, length, brightness, democracy).

4. All nouns which do not fall into one of the above categories are
common nouns. It is not necessary to memorise these categories,
though they are an aid to understanding the nature of the noun.
See also **possessive**, **singular**.

noun clause. See **clause 2 (c)**.

nowhere sometimes occurs as part of a **double negative**:

I can't find it nowhere.

is incorrect for

I can't find it anywhere.

number. The expression *a (large) number of* takes a plural verb:
> A large number of spectators *are* expected.
> There *are* a number of different ways of approaching the problem.

This is because even though *a number* is singular, it obviously has a plural force. However, *the number of* has a singular verb:
> The number of spectators *was* large.

If in doubt, use *many (of)* + plural noun or pronoun + plural verb:
> There *are* many different ways in which the problem can be approached.

O

object. See **accusative, pronoun, verb 4**.

obligate(d) does not mean the same as *oblige(d)*, and should not be used as if it did. It should be confined to legal language.

oblivious to should be *oblivious of*. *Oblivious* does not mean *ignorant*, but *forgetful, unmindful*, etc.

observation and **observance** have different meanings. The former means *taking notice, keeping watch*, etc. The latter means *attending to and performing duty, law, rules, customs, ritual*, etc. *Observation* has nothing to do with performing or complying; *observance* has nothing to do with noticing or watching.

occasion(al) is often mis-spelt with one c or double s. Note also *occasionally*.

occur has the past tense *occurred*, with double r.

of his (of hers, etc.), as in *that dog of his*, seems odd: grammar seems to demand *of him*, and *of his* is a double possessive. The usage is, however, accepted idiom. But see **possessive 7**.

off of is common in certain parts of England (*The door came off of its hinges*) and is incorrect, the *of* being redundant.

off-hand or offhand may be both adjective and adverb: *off-handed* and *off-handedly* are unnecessary.

officious (meddlesome, over-zealous, interfering) should not be confused with *official* (properly authorised).

on-going. The popularity of this word has become an epidemic. It is an over-used, pretentious and totally unnecessary substitute for *continuing*, and ought to be shunned.

on to and **onto** have different meanings. *On to* is used when the meanings of the two words are separate, i.e. when *on* is a full adverb (expressing movement), so that *verb*+*on* has an independent force from *to*+*noun/pronoun*. Thus
> Let's walk on to the next village.

but
> Help me lift it onto the bench.
> He struggled on to the end of his speech.

but
> The horse struggled onto its legs again.

Do not use *onto* where *on* or *to* would suffice. *The horse struggled to its legs again* is better.

one 1. If *one* is used in an impersonal construction (i.e. as a substitute for *I, you*, etc.), the construction should be sustained throughout:
> One tries to do one's (*not* our, your, etc.) best.
> One does what one (*not* you, etc.) can.
> If one travels by daily return, one has (*not* you have) to leave before ten o'clock in the morning.

It is necessary to decide whether to use *one ... one* or *you ... you* or *the person ... he*, and persist with the chosen construction. However, the *one ... one* construction can become cumbersome and affected if carried to any length, and is best left to royalty.
2. If *one* is used numerically, the personal pronouns that follow should be *he* (doing duty for *he or she*) and *his* (doing duty for *his or hers*):
> One of the passengers has left *his* suitcase (*not* their) in the bar.

3. *One* has the possessive *one's*.
See also **one in, one of**.

one another. See **each other**.

one in. Note the singular verb in
> One in nine rate-payers *is* in arrears.

because the subject of the verb is *one*, a singular word. But *two in nine are ...*

one of, followed by a plural noun or pronoun, is a frequent cause of error, because it encourages a singular verb:
> She is one of those athletes who *is* never satisfied with her performance.

A moment's thought will show that she is *one* of a group of *athletes who are never satisfied with their performance*. A similar error occurs in
> It must be one of the most repulsive books that has ever been published.

Here *has* should be *have*.

one of, if not the ... Attempts to reconcile two different grammatical structures in one sentence are found in such sentences as
> The new National Theatre is one of the most imaginative, if not the most imaginative, buildings of our time.

But the parenthetical *if not the most imaginative* needs *building*, not *buildings*, to complete it, and the sentence needs to be recast:
> The new National Theatre is one of the most imaginative buildings of our time, if not the most imaginative of all.

Or
> The new National Theatre is one of the most imaginative, if not the most imaginative, of the buildings of our time.

There are many variations on this problem and its solution, but all solutions must satisfy two criteria:

(*a*) any parenthesis should accord with the grammatical structure of the rest of a sentence.

(*b*) a sentence must make grammatical sense if any parenthesis is removed.

ongoing. See **on-going**.

only must be carefully placed, close to the word it belongs to. Note:

1. *The local wine-merchant loans glasses for weddings.*
2. *Only the local wine-merchant* (as distinct from any other wine-merchants) *loans glasses for weddings.*
3. *The local wine-merchant only loans* (i.e. he does not sell or give away) *glasses for weddings.*
4. *The local wine-merchant loans only glasses* (and nothing else) *for weddings.*
5. *The local wine-merchant loans glasses only for weddings* (and for no other functions).

There is little point in insisting that *You only live once* should be *You live only once*: the meaning is perfectly clear. There is ambiguity, however, in
> The noise can only be reduced by sound-proofing.

onomatopoeia

Does this mean *only reduced* (i.e. not eliminated), or *reduced only by sound-proofing* (i.e. not by double-glazing, etc.)? In conversation, the intended meaning could be communicated by emphasis in the voice: in writing, the meaning must be expressed by the correct order of words.

Note that *only*=solely, exclusively. It is used nonsensically in
We never write, only at Christmas.
where *only* should be *except*.

onomatopoeia is the use of words whose sounds echo their sense:
Only the stuttering rifles' rapid rattle
Can patter out their hasty orisons.

(Wilfred Owen)

onto. See **on to**.

operative word is a common expression in which *operative* is used to mean *most important*. This is a misuse; *operative* means *having effect*, as in
The law is no longer operative in parts of the country.

opportunity should be followed by *of*, not *to*, as in
You will have an opportunity of visiting ... (*not* to visit).

opposite as an adjective takes *to* (or *from*), as in
The Minister took the opposite view to that expressed by his advisers.
As a noun, *opposite* takes *of*:
The verdict was the opposite of what had been expected.

optimal is an alternative to *optimum* (adjective). See **optimum**.

optimism. The dictionary definition is interesting and little-known: '*doctrine* ... that the actual world is the best of all possible worlds; *view* that good must ultimately prevail over evil in the universe; sanguine *disposition*; *inclination* to take bright views' (*C.O.D.*). The italicised words show that optimism is *habitual*, and that to describe a man as optimistic is to say that he *always* has a certain outlook. Strictly speaking, therefore, it is wrong to use *optimism* or *optimistic* when referring to particular, not habitual, circumstances, as in
The Council is worried by the lack of public support,

but is optimistic that, in the long term, its plans will be
seen to have been justified.

Here *hopeful* or *sanguine* would have been correct. In short, *optimism, optimist*, etc., should denote a habitual frame of mind, not a
temporary one.

optimum, as an adjective, means *most favourable*, not – as is sometimes thought – *biggest, highest*, etc. The *optimum size* of a comprehensive school is the size at which it can operate most effectively.
The *optimum speed* of a vehicle is not its top speed but the speed at
which various conflicting factors – passenger comfort, economy
and engine-wear, as well as rapidity – are reconciled. The *optimum
use* does NOT mean the *most use*, but the best.

Optimum as a noun means *most favourable conditions*.

or. Note the singular verb in
      Heavy frost or even snow *is* (not *are*) expected ...
because the sense is that frost *is* expected or snow *is*. But *frost and
snow are expected*. The rules governing the use of *or* are the same as
those for **either ... or**.

Or should not be used where *nor* would be correct. It is necessary to use *nor* after *neither*, and the following is wrong:
      The train had neither restaurant or snack-bar.
See **either ... or, neither ... nor, nor**.

or so. See **or two**.

or two added to a noun needs a plural verb (*A spoonful or two are required*), but *or so* added to a singular noun needs a singular verb (*A
spoonful or so is required*), since *or so* in such a context means
approximately and does not alter the singularity of the subject.

oral: spoken; by word of mouth. See **verbal**.

order, as in *in order that*. See **may 3**.

orientate means *turn in a specified direction*. To *orientate oneself* is to
find one's bearings.

The word is over-used, sometimes pretentiously, and deserves a
rest. An *orientation course* is merely a training course. In
      The series of lessons will *be orientated towards* the needs
      of beginners.
the italicised words mean simply *be directed at* or *try to meet*.

Note that the verb *orient* means exactly the same as *orientate*, and
is shorter.

other

other is sometimes misused, as in *Every other village but this one has main drainage*, which should be *Every village but this one* ... The word *other* is superfluous in view of the rest of the sentence.

See also **otherwise**.

other than is adjectival, never adverbial. The following adverbial uses are incorrect, and should have *except* (or *otherwise than*):

He could not have succeeded *other than* by hard work.

Bookings cannot be made *other than* on the day of the flight.

other than that is adjectival.

Correct: I'd prefer some other colour than that.

Incorrect: Other than that, I'm quite satisfied.

which should have *Apart from that*.

See also **other than, than**.

otherwise is always an adverb, and is wrongly used in

There are objections, both administrative and otherwise.

What is at issue is the merits or otherwise of long-distance weather-forecasting.

What is needed here is not the adverb *otherwise*, but, in the first sentence, an adjective to balance *administrative*: *other* would be correct, and if this sounds odd the writer should have been more specific. In the second sentence, a noun is necessary to balance *merits*: probably *demerits* was meant.

Problems of this sort occur when *and otherwise* and *or otherwise* are tacked on to nouns and adjectives to denote their opposites. The only correct use of *otherwise* is as an adverb:

He could not have acted otherwise.

See also **than**.

ought is the only form of the verb: the past tense is indicated by the use of *ought*+a perfect infinitive, as in

The doctor ought to have forseen the danger.

For an explanation of perfect infinitive, see **verb 5 (a)**.

Ought and *should* have similar meanings but *ought* is the stronger word, implying a greater degree of obligation than *should* does.

ours is never spelt *our's*. See **pronoun 3**.

outside of is incorrect for *outside* in

Wait for me outside of the library.

The vet is not available outside of normal working hours.

Though such use is common, it should be regarded as colloquial.

There is, of course, no objection to *outside + of* when *outside* is a noun:

> The outside of the building is less attractive than the interior.

outward and **outwards** mean the same (*in an outward direction; towards what is outside*) when they are adverbs. Only *outward*, however, is an adjective, as in *the outward side*, and occasionally a noun.

overall is grossly over-used, and can usually be omitted without making the slightest difference to the sense. Its current popularity shows in the frequency with which it is added, almost instinctively, invariably superfluously, in such phrases as *overall cost, overall picture, overall deficit, overall receipts, overall spending, overall policy*, etc.

Gowers lists about a dozen and a half quotations in which some alternative to *overall* could have been more precise and less predictable: the alternatives include *total, average, aggregate, on the whole, over-riding, generally, comprehensive, whole, complete, absolute* and *on balance*.

If *overall* can be omitted, omit it. If a more precise alternative is available, use it.

owing to may be an adjective meaning *caused by*

> His retirement is owing to ill health.

or a preposition meaning *on account of*

> Owing to staff shortage, all trains are running late.

This being so, it is safer to use *owing to* than *due to*, which is less flexible.
See **due to**.

P

p (abbreviation of penny, pence). See **pee**.

p.p. is found at the end of a letter when someone signs it *p.p.* (Latin *per pro*, i.e. on behalf of) another named person, usually a superior. The practice of using *for* instead of *p.p.* is gaining ground, is welcome, and should be encouraged.

pair of. See **singular 4**.

panic has *panicked* and *panicking*.

paragraph: a group of sentences forming a unity by virtue of relating to a single main point which is often announced in the first sentence of the paragraph, the rest of the sentences following in an orderly pattern and developing the theme logically.

No rules governing the length of a paragraph can be laid down. Long paragraphs may confuse the reader; short ones, as usually found in popular newspapers, can produce a jerky, disjointed or breathless effect. Much will depend on the nature of the written material, be it narrative, argument, description, or whatever. The best rule is to begin a new paragraph when the introduction of a new development demands a more distinct break than a full stop can supply. Paragraphing is in fact a form of punctuation.

A new paragraph is normally marked by setting the first word away from the margin (i.e. by *indenting* it).

For other rules of paragraphing, see **quotation marks 1**.

parallel is frequently mis-spelt. Note also that the final *l* is not doubled when forming such words as *unparalleled*.

parameter is an abstruse mathematical term which does NOT mean *perimeter*. It has become, in the plural, a fashionable and unnecessary substitute for *limits, constraints, boundaries* or *conditions*, and should be avoided by those who value plain speaking more than an ostentatious show of inaccurate learning.

paranoia is a mental illness usually marked by delusions of grandeur. English is cheapened (and mental illness is mocked) if the word is used as a loose or jocular alternative to *pomposity* or *suspicion of others' motives*.

parenthesis. See **brackets** and **dash**.

partial means
    (i) *biased, unfair*, as in
        The referee was partial (i.e. not impartial).
    (ii) *having a liking for*, as in
        She is partial to chocolate cake.
    (iii) *incomplete*, as in
        A partial success.
For confusion of *partially* with *partly*, see **partly**.

partial, partiality. One is *partial to* (i.e. has a liking for) someone or something, but one has or shows *partiality for* someone or something.

participle: a verbal adjective, i.e. a word formed from a verb and doing the work of an adjective in describing a noun.

There are two kinds of participle, *present* and *past*. The present participle ends in -ing (*driving*, *referring*). The past participle ends in -d or -ed (*heard*, *walked*), -n (*woven*) or -t (*lent*).

Participles may be used
(a) as adjectives:
 the *rising* sun; *broken* glass.
(b) to form tenses of verbs:
 he had *called*, they were *washing*,
 she is *cooking*, we have been *sent*.
(c) in adjectival phrases:
 The glass, *having been broken*, had to be replaced.
Here the participle is a past participle which is passive (see **active and passive**).
 Not knowing the district, they had difficulty in finding the house.
Here the participle is a present participle describing *they*.

Note the difference between participles (verbal adjectives) and gerunds (verbal nouns). In the following, the italicised words are doing the work of nouns and are therefore gerunds, not participles:
 The hall is not licensed for *dancing*.
 Swimming is forbidden when the red flag is flying.
 The attendant objected to their *feeding* the animals.
For some grammatical difficulties associated with participles, see **verb 5 (b)** and **verb 10**. For a description of the gerund, see **verb 5 (c)**.

particular is often used, especially after *this* and *that*, in a way that adds nothing to the meaning of an expression. Unless it is necessary (it means *relating to one as distinguished from others*; *special*), it should be omitted. It will seldom be found to be necessary after *this, that, his, our*, and other already specific pronouns. Thus *this particular problem* and *your particular enquiry* may mean no more than *this problem* and *your enquiry* do unaided.

partly means *in part*. *Partially* means *incompletely*, and is used wrongly for *partly* in *a soup made partially of meat and partially of vegetables*. In some contexts, however, *partly* and *partially* are interchangeable.

parts of speech are the grammatical classes of words: **adjective**, **adverb**, **conjunction**, **interjection**, **noun**, **preposition**, **pronoun**, **verb**. For full information, see the separate entries under these words.

pass has *passed* as both past tense (*Time passed slowly*) and past participle (*The event has passed unnoticed*). It is necessary to avoid confusion with the similarly pronounced *past*, which may be adjective (*during the past*

passive

week), noun (*in the past*), preposition (*Drive past the shopping-centre*), or adverb (*Four taxis have gone past*). Use *passed* only as a verb.

passive. See **active and passive**.

past. See **pass**.

past participle. See **verb 5 (b)**.

past tense. See **verb 2**.

pathos is the quality (in events, writing, speech, etc.) that excites pity or sadness. It should not be confused with *bathos*, which is anti-climax, a sudden change from the sublime to the ridiculous.

peaceable, peaceful. The former is restricted 'to persons, their character, their actions, their feelings, etc.'; the latter is applied 'to periods, occasions, countries, scenes, parties, states of mind, appearances, faces' (Partridge). Thus *a peaceable nation* with *peaceful intentions* towards its neighbours.

pee. The basic unit of English currency is the *penny* (plural *pence*), both abbreviated to *p* in writing. Since the decimalisation of English currency, there have been few disasters more ugly than the suddenly widespread custom of using this abbreviation as if it were a word, pronounced *pee*:

It costs one pound forty pee.

The effort of saying or writing *pence* (or *penny* where appropriate) is scarcely greater than the effort of saying *pee*, and the reader is invited to repudiate this debasement of the currency.

peer, despite its aristocratic associations, means an *equal*, not a *superior*, in such contexts as

As a song-writer, Schubert has no peer.

Likewise *peerless*, having no equal.

pence. See **pee**.

per means *for each* as in *seventy miles per hour, a hire-charge of eight pounds per week*. Purists prefer the English *a* or *an* (*seventy miles an hour, eight pounds a week*), retaining the Latin *per* for Latin expressions such as *per annum, per capita, per cent*, etc. But see **per annum, per se** and **p.p.**

per annum has the useful abbreviation *p.a.*, but in other circumstances why not use *a year*?

per se means *of, by or in itself*, which are preferable.

percentage. There is no good reason for using this word when *part* would suffice, nor for using *a large percentage of* instead of simply *many* or *most*. Shortness in words is usually a merit.

It is not true that a percentage is always a small part. (*Only a percentage of cars failed to pass the test.*) A percentage can be larger than the whole (e.g. 200%).

perfect tense. See **verb 2**.

perhaps. See **comma 7**.

period of time is unnecessary: *period* on its own is quite sufficient.

person. For an explanation of this grammatical term as applied to pronouns, see the first part of the entry **pronoun**.

Person is also applied to some parts of verbs, but the general reader is likely to encounter it only in the expression *the first person*, meaning *I* or *we*. A piece of writing *in the first person* is autobiographical, with much use of *I*, *me* and *my*.

personal pronoun. See **pronoun**.

personnel, pronounced with the stress on the final syllable, is a *singular* noun meaning *body of persons engaged in some public service or in a factory*, though it may sometimes be used adjectivally as in *personnel manager*, etc. Avoid confusion with *personal*, which has a quite different meaning.

perspicacity: clearness of understanding. *Perspicuity*: clearness of statement. A *perspicacious* person has good mental discernment: a *perspicuous* one expresses himself clearly.

phenomenon has the plural *phenomena*, which is often incorrectly used as if it were a singular. *This phenomena* should be either *this phenomenon* or *these phenomena*.

phrase: a group of words which makes incomplete sense and does not contain a finite verb (see **verb 3**). A phrase can do the work of
    (*a*) a noun (acting as the subject, object or complement of a verb, or as the object of a preposition):
        Walking on the grass is forbidden. (subject)
        The pilot tried *to bale out*. (object)
        The intention is *to keep prices down*. (complement)
        He has the excuse of *being ill*. (object of preposition)
        See **verb 5 (a)** and **5 (c)**.
    (*b*) An adjective (describing a noun or pronoun):
        Having put the cat out, he went to bed.
        See **verb 5 (b)**.

pitiable

(c) an adverb:
Frost is expected *during the night*.

pitiable: deserving pity. *Pitiful*: showing (or feeling) pity (though the word is often used to mean *contemptible* as in a *pitifully small contribution*). Thus
The survivors of the wreck were found in a pitiful condition.
should read *pitiable*.

playwright, not *playwrite*.

plethora. See **dearth**.

pluperfect tense. See **verb 2**.

plural. See **singular**.

point in time, at this. Another example of the modern fashion for using several words when one would suffice. A pretentious way of saying *now*, and perhaps already a cliché.

point of view is an expression that is often used in ugly combinations:
From the exercise point of view, a hand-mower is preferable to an electric one.
The problem is easily avoided:
A hand-mower provides better exercise than an electric one does.
Point of view means *way of looking at a matter*. It is safest to assume that only people (or animals) can 'view' things, and to restrict the use of *point of view* accordingly:
The architect's point of view may be different from the builder's.

polloi. See **hoi polloi**.

poor thing, but my own. Shakespeare wrote (in *As You Like It*)
An ill-favoured thing, sir, but mine own.
and if the words deserve quotation, they deserve correct quotation.

possessive. To express ownership or possession, a noun or pronoun has the *possessive* form (sometimes called the *genitive*):
Henry's football; *our* baggage.
1. For the possessive form of pronouns, see **pronoun**.
2. To form the possessive of a singular noun, add *'s*:
the *team's* results; the *country's* economy.

3. To form the possessive of a plural noun, add just an apostrophe
(') to the normal plural:
> Ladies' hairdresser; *magistrates'* powers; the *Browns'* house.

There is one important exception to this rule. Some nouns do not
have a plural ending in *s*, e.g. woman, *women*; child, *children* – for
other examples see **singular 1 (d), (e)**. Such nouns form the possessive plural by adding *'s* to the normal plural:
> *men's* department; *sheep's* heads.

4. Some names ending in *s* may take an apostrophe alone, rather
than *'s*, in the possessive:
> Dickens' novels; King Charles' spaniels.

though *Dickens's* and *Charles's* would be equally correct. *For goodness' sake* is correct.

5. In such expressions as
> I'm going to my cousin's.

the apostrophe is needed to denote that *cousin's* is short for *cousin's
home*, and is not a straightforward plural. If one is going to stay
with more than one cousin, write
> I'm going to my cousins'.

or
> I'm going to stay with my cousins.

No apostrophe is needed in this second example because *cousins* is
a simple plural, not an abbreviation for *cousins' house*.

6. It is possible to regard a short phrase as a single unit and add the
apostrophe to the final word even though that word may not be
the actual or the only 'possessor':
> the King of Spain's beard; my aunt and uncle's arrival;
> Hodder and Stoughton's catalogue.

7. Avoid the ungrammatical double possessive
> The President's policy appears to be more liberal than
> that of Mr Nixon's.

which should read either
> ... than that of Mr Nixon.

or
> than Mr Nixon's.

It is, of course, possible to express possession by using *of* instead
of an apostrophe:
> The policy of the President *or* The President's policy.

It is not possible to use both of these methods at once.

8. Note the correct use of the apostrophe in
> a good day's work; a year's supply; a month's holiday;
> the week's washing.

pound

where the idea of possession is present, if not very obviously: the
work *of* a day, a supply *for* a year, etc.

pound has the plural *pounds*. The use of *pound* as a plural is common
(*He earns sixty pound a week*) but colloquial, except in combinations
such as *a five-pound fine, a fourteen-pound bag of potatoes*, which are Standard English.

practicable: feasible. *Practical*: useful; concerned with practice (rather
than theory); practising; inclined to action rather than speculation.
Practical is often used where *practicable* would have been correct,
as in
> They would have liked to invite all their friends to the
> wedding, but it wasn't practical.

A *practicable plan* is one capable of being put into practice. A *practical
plan* is one with a stress on practicalities rather than theories.
See **impracticable**.

practical. See **practicable**.

practical proposition. A common and long-winded expression, and
probably wrong for *a practicable proposition* (see **practicable**). If something is not *a practical proposition*, it is merely not *possible*.

practice and **practise** are very frequently confused. *Practice* is the noun,
practise the verb. The difference may be remembered by analogy with
advice (noun) and *advise* (verb), the spellings of which are helpfully
in accordance with normal rules of pronunciation.

precede means *go before*, but *proceed* means *go on*.

precedence and **precedent** are sometimes confused. *Precedence* is
priority, superiority, as in
> The saving of human life takes precedence over the
> saving of property.

Precedent: previous case taken as example or justification for subsequent cases:
> There is no precedent (*or* There are no precedents) for a
> wage-claim of this magnitude.

precipitate. See **precipitous**.

precipitous: very steep. The word is frequently and ludicrously confused with the adjective *precipitate* (rash, violently hurried), as in

The Chancellor's mini-budget appears to have been
precipitously assembled.

prefer is followed by *to*, never by *than*:
He prefers a pipe *to* cigarettes.

However, when *prefer* is followed, as it often is, by an infinitive, *rather
than* is an acceptable alternative to *to*:
He preferred to emigrate *rather than* (to) pay this
country's taxes.

But *than* on its own is never correct. The following is therefore
wrong:
He preferred to emigrate than pay this country's taxes.
Prefer means *like better*. Thus
I prefer this colour better.

is wrong because *prefer ... better* is ungrammatical, the *better* being
redundant. Say simply *I prefer this colour* or *I like this colour better*.
See **preferable to, than**.

preferable to, never *preferable than*.
Gas is preferable *to* electricity.

If *preferable* is followed by an infinitive, as it often is, *rather than* is
an acceptable alternative to *to*:
It is preferable to use gas rather than (to use) electricity.
But *than* on its own is never correct.

Since *preferable* means *liked better*, it is as ungrammatical to say *more
preferable* as to say *more better*.

Preferable is pronounced with the stress on the first syllable, not the
second.

prefix: verbal element placed at the beginning of a word to qualify the
meaning. In English, most prefixes are from Latin or Greek. Some
examples:

Prefix	Meaning	Example
inter	between	interfere, intervention
re	again, back	reconstruct, reproduction
un	not	uncover, undamaged.

Other common prefixes include *ad* (to), *ante* (before), *bene* (good),
bi (twice), *co* (together), *de* (down), *ex* (out of), *in* (into, not), *mis*
(wrongly), *proto* (first), *poly* (many), *post* (after), *pre* (before), *sub*
(under), *syn* (together), *trans* (across), *tri* (triple).

premises, not *premisses*.

preposition: a word used with a noun (or noun equivalent, e.g.

preposition

a pronoun or gerund) to denote the noun's relationship to some other word. The importance of prepositions may be seen in the following two sentences, the differences of meaning between which are caused entirely by prepositions:

> We went *down* the path, *over* the fence and *across* the field.
> We went *up* the path, *under* the fence and *round* the field.

The second sentence carries a meaning different from that of the first because the prepositions express different relationships between the various nouns (path, fence, field) and the verb (went).

A preposition usually precedes the noun.

1. A preposition may link a noun (or noun equivalent) with
(*a*) a verb:

> It *sank during* an unexpected squall. (*i.e. expressing relationship between* squall *and* sank)

(*b*) an adjective:

> *Weary with* fatigue, they set off home. (i.e. *expressing relationship between* weary *and* fatigue)

(*c*) another noun or pronoun:

> This is the best *bargain of* all. (i.e. *expressing relationship between* bargain *and* all)

2. If a preposition is followed by a pronoun, the pronoun must be in the accusative (if it has one). See **pronoun**.

> Invitations have been sent to *them* and *us*.
> There was too much for my wife and *me* to eat.
> *Whom* would you like to sit with?
> Between you and *me*, I think it's a bad idea.

3. In order to identify a preposition, consider its function in a sentence. Unless a word is expressing relationship as defined above, it is not a preposition.

> The argument went *over* my head. (preposition)
> He fell *over*. (adverb)
> Water flooded *down* the hill. (preposition)
> We all have our ups and *downs*. (noun)
> Come *down*! (adverb)
> What time shall we *down* tools? (verb)

4. It has sometimes been said that a sentence should not end with a preposition. This is a rule that is difficult to justify. There are occasions when a final preposition is clumsy or ambiguous: there are likewise occasions when attempts to avoid a final preposition cause inelegance or confusion. Clarity and grace should be the aim,

not pedantic adherence to an untenable view that, because the word preposition comes from the Latin for *placed before*, a preposition can never be last. Sir Winston Churchill is said to have written

This is the sort of English up with which I will not put.

to ridicule the clumsiness which can occur as a result of attempts to avoid final prepositions. No-one could possibly object to

This is something I will not put *up with*.

present participle. See **verb 5 (b)**.

present tense. See **verb 2**.

presumptuous. See **pretentious**.

pretentious. The *-tious* is pronounced *-shus*. *Presumptuous*, however, is pronounced as spelt.

preventive, not *preventative*, is the normal word. It means *serving to prevent*, as in *preventive medicine*, which is medicine designed to prevent illness (as distinct from medicine designed to cure an already existing illness).

previously. See **ago**.

primarily is pronounced with the stress on the first syllable. Pronunciation with the stress on the second is American.

principal and **principle** are very often confused. *Principal* means *chief*. It may be an adjective (remember 'a for adjective' in the final syllable) meaning *first in importance*, as in *my principal reason for coming*. It may be a noun (remember the final syllable *pal* is a noun) meaning *person in charge*, as in *the principal of the college*.

Principle means *general law* or *code of right conduct*, and is always a noun: *a man of principle*; *the invention works on the principle that* . . .

prise, pry. The former (which may be spelt *prize*) means *force by leverage*: a burglar may *prise open* a window with a jemmy. The verb *pry* means *peer inquisitively* or *inquire impertinently*.

Literate housewives have recently experienced difficulty following their purchase, from a major company, of meat-paste in containers bearing the puzzling instruction PRY OPEN.

proceed. The noun is *procedure*, with one *e*. Note also *precede*.

productivity 'is a horrible word; use *output*' (Partridge).

professional: an interesting example of a word which lost its original meaning, and has subsequently lost virtually all its meaning, as a result

proficient

of over-use. A profession used to be a self-governing body of people who controlled their own standards and their own qualifications for admission. Clergymen, doctors and lawyers belonged to professions. Now soldiers, criminals and footballers call themselves *professionals*; footballers even commit *professional fouls*, which may be defined as *deliberate and serious breaches of the rules in order to neutralise an opponent's superior skill*. The noun *professional* has been debased to mean nothing more than *one who earns a living in a particular occupation*.

proficient. See **efficient**.

program. This American spelling is now generally used when the word denotes the instructions fed into a computer. In all other circumstances *programme* is correct.

prone: lying face downwards. *Supine*: lying face upwards.

pronoun: a word used in place of a noun. If words such as *I* and *she*, for example, did not exist, it would be necessary for people's full names to be spoken or written whenever they were referred to. Pronouns are thus very useful short-hand words. The words *I, you, he, she, it, we, they*, are examples of the *personal pronoun*.

Personal pronouns are the only words in English that have different forms depending on whether

(*a*) they are used as the subject of a sentence. Pronouns acting as subject are said to be *in the nominative* (*case*). (Some books refer to this as the subjective case.)

(*b*) they are the object of a verb or preposition. Pronouns acting as object are said to be in the *accusative case*. (Some books refer to this as the objective case.)

(*c*) they indicate possession. Such pronouns are said to be in the *possessive* (or *genitive*) case.

		Nominative	Accusative	Possessive
Singular	*1st Person*	I	me	mine
	2nd Person	you	you	yours
	3rd Person	he, she, it	him, her, it	his, hers, its
Plural	*1st Person*	we	us	ours
	2nd Person	you	you	yours
	3rd Person	they	them	theirs

1. Examples of pronouns in the nominative:

(*a*) as the subject of a verb:

He and *I* agree.

Have *we* misunderstood?

(*b*) as the complement (see **verb 7**) of the intransitive verb *to be*:

112

It is *I* (or *she*, *we*, *they*, etc.) who must take the responsibility.

Such common expressions as *it's me* and *was it them?* are incorrect, because the verb *to be* cannot take the accusative: the correct expressions are *it's I* and *was it they?*. But general usage has led to their acceptance, and even to gentle ridicule of the correct version:

Newcomer at Heaven's Gates: Knock, knock.

St Peter: Who's there?

Newcomer: It is I.

St Peter: Go away. We don't want any more
schoolteachers here.

The expression *It's me* should only be used as an entire sentence; it remains wrong if used as part of a longer sentence, as in

It's me who did it

which should be *It is I who did it*.

2. Examples of pronouns in the accusative:

(*a*) as the object of a verb:

The outcome surprised *them*.

(*b*) as the object of a preposition (see **preposition 2**).

It was a gift from *him* to *them*.

Avoid the very common fault *between you and I*. The *I* should be the accusative *me* after the preposition *between*.

3. The pronoun in the possessive.

(*a*) the possessive forms *yours*, *hers*, *ours*, *its*, *theirs* do not take the apostrophe. The possessive *its* should be distinguished from *it's*, which is an abbreviation of *it is*, the apostrophe denoting an omitted letter. *Theirs* is never spelt *their's*.

(*b*) the possessive forms *my*, *your*, *her*, *our*, *their* are to be regarded as adjectives.

4. In addition to personal pronouns, there are several other categories of pronoun, but it is not necessary to memorise them.

(*a*) Demonstrative pronouns: *that*, *this*, *those*, *these* (but only when used instead of nouns):

Those are the sweets I like.

Compare

Those sweets are the ones I like.

where *those* is a straightforward adjective describing the noun *sweets*.

(*b*) Interrogative pronouns: *who*, *whose*, *whom*, *which*, *what* (but only in questions):

To whom do you wish to speak?

Note the accusative *whom* after the preposition *to*. This unique accusative is widely ignored, as in

Who did you see?

instead of *Whom* . . . , object of the verb *see*. See the longer entry at **whom**. See also **what and which**.

(c) Distributive pronouns: *each, either, neither*:

Either will suit me.

(d) Indefinite pronouns: *all, any, few, many, more, most, some*:

All is not lost. Few doubt it.

(e) Reflexive pronouns: *myself, yourself, himself*, etc. These may refer back to the subject of a sentence

He blamed himself.

or be used simply for emphasis:

I saw it myself.

They must not be used as substitutes for straightforward personal pronouns:

My brother and myself are keen bird-watchers.

should read

My brother and I . . .

The use of such reflexive pronouns instead of personal pronouns is very widespread, and is incorrect. The use of *myself* instead of *I* or *me* is particularly prevalent.

5. To identify parts of speech, it is always necessary to decide what *function* a word has in a sentence. Here are some of the above words used not as pronouns, but as adjectives:

These bowls are too small.

Which (*What*) page have you reached?

Every cloud has a silver lining.

All men are equal.

The italicised words are adjectives because they are describing nouns, not standing on their own as pronouns.

6. An important category of pronoun is the *relative pronoun*. Relative pronouns include *who* (*whom, whose*), *which* and *that*. (See separate entry for **that**.)

The sentence

We gave advice and our advice was ignored.

may be rewritten

We gave advice *which* was ignored.

Here, *which* replaces *and our advice*. It therefore acts as a pronoun (standing for the noun *advice*) and also as a conjunction (replacing *and*). A relative pronoun does the work of a pronoun and also joins clauses together (see **clause**).

Other examples:

(a)   We did not hear the postman. He was knocking.
    This could be rewritten
        We did not hear the postman *who* was knocking.
    Here the relative pronoun *who* replaces the full stop and the
    pronoun *He*. It does not replace any conjunction but does the
    work of a conjunction in joining two sentences previously
    separated by a full stop and making them into one sentence.

(b)   You need a driving instructor *whom* you have confidence
    in (*or* in whom you have confidence).
    The accusative *whom* is necessary with the preposition *in*, though
    whom is a word strangely shunned by most English people.

(c)   The islanders, whose rights had been infringed, took the
    matter to the International Court.
    Expressed as two separate statements, this becomes
        The islanders' rights had been infringed.
        The islanders took the matter to the International Court.
    The possessive *whose* is needed in the single-sentence version
    because it replaces the possessive form *the islanders'* in the second
    version.

7. It is common for the relative pronoun to be omitted:
    Follow the path (which) you took yesterday.
    This is the friend (whom) I was telling you about.

8. Prounouns can cause confusion or error.

(a)   The prisoner told the judge that he was an idiot.
    He the prisoner or he the judge? Ambiguity of this kind, stem-
    ming from the careless use of a pronoun, is to be avoided.

(b)   The England team is the worst for years, and they cannot
    expect to win the Championship.
    The collective noun *team* may be singlular or plural. Here the
    writer has chosen the singular, as can be seen from the singular
    verb *is*. That being so, it is wrong then to switch to the plural
    pronoun *they*. Either keep the whole sentence singular (by
    changing *they* to *it*) or put it all into the plural (by changing
    is to *are*). It is ungrammatical to muddle the two. See also **singu-
    lar 6**.

(c)   Everyone must do their best.
    Everyone is singular, and should therefore have the singular *his*
    (which does duty for *his or her*) instead of the plural *their*. The
    lack of a single English word for the clumsy *his or her* often causes
    the adoption of *their* when a singular would be correct.

9. Relative pronouns must be carefully placed. As a general rule,

115

a clause introduced by a relative pronoun should be placed close
to the word to which it relates, as in

The *scheme, which* began last April, involved the
appointment of police liaison *officers who* were to be
called in to advise.

The following (quoted as a correct sentence in a recently published
guide to good English) is intelligible but clumsy:

Smog consists of poisonous exhaust gases from *cars,
which* collect over towns.

10. A pronoun should not be used unless there is a noun or noun-
equivalent that the pronoun stands for.

Council workers have asked that their salaries should be
paid direct into bank accounts, but the Borough
Treasurer has refused to agree to *it.*

The general sense is clear, but what does *it* refer to? Presumably the
council workers' request. But the noun *request* does not appear in
the sentence, nor does any singular noun to which *it* can refer.
The sentence should be corrected by changing *it* to *this request.*
11. One pronoun should not stand for two different things in the
same sentence:

In the absence of any information about the accident, it
is idle to speculate about it.

The first *it* stands for *to speculate,* the second for either *accident* or
information. This is loose English.

See **and which, nobody, that, what and which, which of the
two, whom**.

proper noun. See **noun**.

prophecy (with the *y* pronounced as in *property*) is the noun. *Prophesy*
(with the *y* pronounced as in *by*) is the verb. The rule '*c* for the noun,
s for the verb' may be remembered by reference to *advice* and *advise*.

proportion. The expression *a proportion of,* having five syllables, inevitably tempts some users of English to assume that *some,* having only
one syllable, is necessarily inferior. This is not so. Nor are *many* and
few inferior to the more impressive *in a large/small proportion of.*

Furthermore, the word *proportion* is too often used where *part*
would suffice, the shorter word being, as usual in English, more
powerful than the longer.

proposition is a popular maid-of-all-work which is used to mean *proposal* (a business proposition), *problem* (a tough proposition), *task* (a
stiff proposition), *undertaking* (a paying proposition), *opponent* (a diffi-

cult proposition), *possibility* (a commercial proposition), *method* (a novel proposition), etc. To use one word for so many purposes leads to slackness of expression; *proposition* deserves to be restricted to mean *statement*, *assertion*, and otherwise to be avoided in favour of more precise alternatives.

protagonist does NOT mean *advocate* (of a cause, etc.) or *supporter*. The prefix *proto-* signifies *first, chief, original*, etc. (as in *prototype*), and *protagonist* means *the most prominent person*. There is sometimes confusion with *antagonists*, which means *adversaries*.

Purists claim that there can be only one protagonist, and would object to

The Alpine Club sent a weighty letter to the three
protagonists, appealing for a truce.

Such an objection would be rather pedantic, though *antagonists* may have been intended in the sentence quoted.

protest, as a verb, is used in America to mean *protest against*:

The demonstrators were protesting increased
expenditure on armaments.

This usage is infiltrating the vocabulary of the young in Britain, where it is incorrect.

protrude means *stick out* (the *pro* is from the Latin for *in front of*) and so the expression *protrude out* is ungrammatical and an example of **tautology**.

proximity means *nearness*. *In close* (i.e. near) *proximity to* is therefore repetitious, an example of **tautology**. The single word *near* is enough.

psychological moment is perhaps an acceptable expression when it signifies 'the moment at which a person is in a favourable state of mind (such as a skilled psychologist could choose) for one's dealings with him to produce the effect one desires' (Fowler), though *right moment* will normally suffice, and additionally avoid what has now become a cliché. However, the phrase *at the psychological moment* has come to mean merely *at the right time, at a convenient time, in the nick of time*. As such, it is unnecessary, inaccurate, pretentious and overworked. See **cliché**.

punctuation. The golden rule is to use no more punctuation than is necessary to point the meaning. Clarity of expression depends mainly on the choice of the right words and on their arrangement in the right order. Punctuation exists to help the reader by pointing out the natural groupings of the words used, and to save him the time that, in the absence of punctuation, would have to be spent on re-reading.

See **apostrophe, brackets, comma, dash, exclamation mark, full stop, hyphen, question mark, quotation marks, semicolon**.

purposely, purposefully. The former means *on purpose, not by accident*; the latter means *full of purpose, having a definite intention*. Confusion between the two is illustrated in

> He dominated the meeting from the moment he walked purposely on to the platform.

push, in the military sense of *advance*, is favoured by newspapers because of its brevity, with some curious consequences:

> The rebels pushed down the mountain into the town.
> EIGHTH ARMY PUSH BOTTLES UP GERMANS.

Q

quantative does not exist: the word is *quantitative*.

question. See **beg the question**.

question mark. A question mark is used when there is exact quotation of the actual words of a question:

> What time is it?
> Will there ever be a time when wars will cease?

It may be used, though it is not necessary, when making a request:

> Will you please send me your latest catalogue?

The question mark must not be used if a question is asked indirectly:

> I asked him what the time was.
> I wonder if there will ever be a time when wars will cease.
> I should be glad if you would send me your latest catalogue.

The question mark is the equivalent of a full stop, and should be followed by a new sentence except sometimes when it occurs in **direct speech**.

question whether, not *question of whether* or *question as to whether*, is correct in such contexts as

> The question whether a breach of security occurred will be considered by the Cabinet.

The question is bound to be asked whether it makes commercial sense to manufacture yet another small car.

questionnaire may be pronounced *kweschon-air* or *kestyon-air*. The former is preferable.
The word has been imported from France, and it is true that the second pronunciation is more French. However, the word is now so firmly established in English vocabulary that there is no reason for not pronouncing the *question-* part in the normal English way.

quick. The adverbial forms may be *quickly* (*more quickly*, *most quickly*) or *quick* (*quicker*, *quickest*). The latter are, unusually, identical with the adjectival forms. Thus it is correct to say *Come quick* or *Come quickly.* The *quickly* forms, however, should be used with participles:
>Night is *falling* quickly.
>The quarrel was quickly *forgotten*.
and in all cases when in doubt.

quotation marks, sometimes called *inverted commas* or *speech marks*.
1. These are used to punctuate **direct speech**, i.e. the quotation of the actual words or thoughts of a speaker or writer. It is the modern custom to use single inverted commas (' ... '), though double ones (" ... ") are not incorrect. Note the placing of punctuation in
>The spokesman said, 'No comment.'
>'No comment?' said the journalist, incredulously.
>'That's what I said!' insisted the spokesman. 'No comment.'
>'Call yourself a spokesman,' said another journalist, 'and you've nothing to say?'
>'No comment.'

All the rules for the punctuation of direct speech are exemplified in this extract. Note that it is necessary to begin a new paragraph for each new speaker.
2. For a quotation within a quotation, double inverted commas are used:
>'I cannot agree with the questioner's use of the word "catastrophic". I would describe the position as merely troublesome,' said the Prime Minister.
3. In handwritten documents, it is customary (but not necessary) to put quotation marks round the titles of books, films, etc., though it is common to use underlining in typescript, and italics in print.
4. When a word or group of words is quoted (from, say, a book

or newspaper), quotation marks should be used, but no further punctuation (of the kind used with direct speech) is necessary:

> What Marxists call 'the repressive maintenance of the social hierarchy' in schools is what most people would call good discipline.

A longer quotation of several sentences is best placed in a separate paragraph, usually introduced by a colon, and indented from the margin to make it stand out from normal paragraphs.

5. Inverted commas are sometimes used to indicate that a word is being used mockingly, cynically or light-heartedly, as if *so-called* were being inserted before the word so used: *the 'liberation' of Hungary and Czechoslovakia by the Russians*. This is a useful occasional device, to be used sparingly.

R

racial, racialist, racist. Race relations are delicate matters, and their vocabulary is correspondingly complex and shifting. *Racial* = having to do with race (*racial discrimination*), but it is usually applied to matters involving people with black or dark brown skins. *Ethnic* also = having to do with race (*ethnic differences*), but it is usually applied to matters involving people with yellow or 'white' faces, usually minority groups with common characteristics within a larger community, e.g. Chinese, Irish, Jews in England. *Racialist* (noun and adjective) indicates antagonism between races. The newer variant *racist* means the same, but indicates a greater degree of contempt on the part of the user of the word.

raise is a transitive verb (see **verb 4**): *rise* (*rose, risen*) is intransitive (see **verb 6**).

An increase in wages is a *rise*. The use of *raise* in this sense is an Americanism.

An interesting lunacy is perpetrated by the Cambridge economist who wrote

> Queues could be eliminated if prices were *raised upwards* for goods such as motor-cars.

rare. See **scarce**.

rather is sometimes used loosely.
>He was rather a tall man.

should be
>He was a rather tall man.

because *rather* (somewhat) describes *tall*, not *a tall*.
>He is rather a bore.

is, however, an accepted idiom.

re-. This prefix often has the sense of *again* (rearrange, repeat, recur) or *back* (revert, return) and one must therefore be careful not to add *again* or *back* to verbs beginning *re* if the result will be **tautology**.

react on, reaction on should be used with care. *Reaction* is not the same as *action*. Something may *act on* something else, but something may only *react on* itself. Where *reaction* means *response*, use *reaction to*. Thus
>The news has had a strange *reaction on* public opinion.

is incorrect: news can only *react on* itself. The sentence should be either
>Public opinion has had a strong reaction (*or* has reacted strongly) *to* the news.

or
>The news has had a strong effect on public opinion.

A *reaction* is usually immediate. A response which is not immediate should not be described as a reaction but as an opinion, view or response.

read where should be *read that* in
>Did you read where the Prime Minister has been
>visiting coal-mines near Doncaster?

real. See **adverb 4**; *real* and *really* are often used when they add little or nothing to what is being said. *Really* is probably used unnecessarily more often than not.

realistic means *concerned with, or characterised by, a practical view of life* and should not be used when *reasonable* or *feasible* would be more precise, as in *a realistic price*.

reason should be followed by *that*, not *because*, in such contexts as
>The reason he was absent was because he was ill.

Because means *for the reason that*, and thus the above sentence means
>The reason he was absent was for the reason that he was
>ill.

The correct version is either
>The reason he was absent was that he was ill.

recollect

or

> He was absent because he was ill.

See also **due to**.

recollect and **remember** are often used interchangeably, but there is a difference in shade of meaning which is worth preserving, in that *recollect* means *succeed in remembering*, i.e. the act of remembering is more difficult, less spontaneous, than that expressed by *remember*.

recourse, resort, resource. *Recourse* (in which *-course* is pronounced as in *of course*) is usually found in *have recourse to*, meaning *adopt as adviser, helper or expedient*. As a noun, *recourse* is also found in such phrases as *without recourse to*, i.e. without turning to (a source of help), and *the only recourse*, i.e. the only action (in turning to a source of help). *Recourse* always has the sense of *turning to* or *adopting* a possible source of help.

Resort: that which is turned to for aid, i.e. that to which recourse is had. As a verb, *resort to* means *have recourse to*. The words *recourse* and *resort* therefore have much in common, though one is more likely to say *in the last resort*, not *in the last recourse*. *Without recourse to armed force* and *without resorting to armed force* are more common than *without resort to armed force*, though this is correct.

Resource (with *-source* pronounced *source*): stock that can be drawn on. It is found in such phrases as *without resources, to have no resources*.

The common error is to use *resource* where one of the former two words would have been correct.

recur doubles the *r* for *recurred, recurrence*, etc.

Note that *recur again* is ungrammatical because *recur* means *occur again*, i.e. the idea of *again* is contained in the *re-* of *recur* (as it is in *repeat, rebuild, reconsider, reproduce*, etc.) and so the *again* in *recur again* is superfluous. See **tautology**.

reference. See **regard**.

referendum. Both *referenda* and *referendums* are found as plurals. The latter is to be preferred.

refute means *prove the falsity or error of* (a statement, opinion, argument or person advancing it); *rebut or repel by argument*. It should not be used, as it often is, to mean simply *deny*. The notion of successful counter-argument, not merely denial, should be present when *refute* is used.

See **deny**.

regard. Popular phrases such as *in regard to, with regard to* or *as regards* are often wordy or inexact substitutes for *of, about, in, to* or *for*, as in

> Problems in regard to undermanning in the Police Force were the subject of discussion at the Home Office yesterday.

Here, *of* would have been both shorter and more precise (and *the subject of discussions* could have been expressed in the single word *discussed*).

A similar preference for the longer, more impressive and less exact phrase is often found in the use of *with reference to, in respect of, in relation to, in terms of* and *in connexion with*. These should be used sparingly, and the more simple, less hazy prepositions *of, over, with, to,* etc., should be preferred.

regarding. See **verb 10**.

regards. The phrase *as regards to* is wrong: say simply *as regards*. It is however, correct to say *in/with/without/ regard to*. But see **regard**.

regrettable: deserving of regret. *Regretful:* full of regret. Thus a *regrettable accident* and a *regretful culprit*.

reiterate. *Iterate* means *repeat*. The prefix *re-* means, among other things, *once more, again, anew, afresh, repeated*. Therefore *reiterate* means *repeat more than once*, i.e. say more than twice. *Reiterate* is often (indeed usually) used as if it meant *repeat*, and some dictionaries now state that the two words mean the same. *Reiterate* is seldom superior to *repeat*, however, except in the eyes of those caught up in the modern habit of always preferring the longer word to the shorter.

relation to. See **regard**.

relation(s) with, not *relation(s) towards*.

relative pronoun. See **pronoun 6**.

relatively is often used unthinkingly. It should be used only when a standard of comparison has been stated or is implied.

> I have a relatively small car.

means that the car is small in relation to other cars, but *small* means precisely that without the aid of *relatively*, which is being wrongly used to mean *fairly*. The word *relatively* should have been omitted. But

> The Inspector of Taxes replied relatively quickly.

means not that he replied quickly, but that he replied quickly by the standards of promptness one had come to expect from him. This is a legitimate use of *relatively*: its omission would alter the sense.

relevant

relevant is mispronounced *revelant* with curious frequency.

remediable, remedial. The former means *capable of being remedied*; *curable*. The latter means *providing a remedy*. Remedial education is that designed to remedy special learning difficulties, though not all of them may be remediable.

rent means *occupy or use in return for paying money*. It is correct to say that the owner of a property *rents* it (*out*) to someone, but why use *rent* (*out*) in this way, as the opposite of *rent* as originally defined, when *let* is available?

repairable and its opposite *unrepairable*, both pronounced with the emphasis on -*pair*, are applied to physical things such as cars and shoes. *Reparable* and *irreparable*, pronounced with the emphasis on *rep*, are best reserved for abstract things such as loss and harm, as in *irreparable damage to relations between the two countries*.

reparable. See **repairable**.

repeat. See **again**.

repetition. The repetition of words or sounds is regarded as ugly style in writing:

> There is a poss*ibility* that his in*ability* ...
> *Of* many *of* those men, *of* whom few are still alive, it
> can be said that ...

replica means *copy, duplicate or reproduction of a work of art*, made, strictly speaking, by the original artist. As Fowler sensibly points out, the word is worth retaining in this unique sense. Otherwise (e.g. when referring to copies by other artists or to modern reproductions) use *copy, duplicate* or *reproduction*. The following, from an *Observer* review of a television documentary about an eighteenth century engineer, illustrates the misuse:

> Constructing a replica of his engine, exalted artisans
> showed by their faces that he was a man to be
> wondered at.

replies to invitations. A formal invitation is likely to be impersonal in style:

> Mr and Mrs — request the pleasure of the company of
> Mr and Mrs — at the wedding of their daughter ...

The reply may be similarly impersonal:

> Mr and Mrs — thank Mr and Mrs — for their kind
> invitation to ... on ... at ... o'clock and are pleased to
> accept.

Such a reply would not be signed. Alternatively, a more informal reply in the form of a letter is acceptable if the host and hostess are friends. See **letter writing**.

reported speech is the same as **indirect speech**.

requirement and **requisite** (as a noun) are frequently synonymous. *Requirement* is the more general word, and can be applied to both abstract and concrete needs. *Requisite* is properly *thing needed*, and is thus wrongly used in

It's only a small cooker, but it meets all our requisites.

If in doubt, use *requirement*, which embraces the meanings of *requisite*. See also **tautology**.

research in or **into** is better than *on*.

resort. See **recourse**.

resource. See **recourse**.

respect. See **regard**.

respectable, respectful. The former means *deserving respect*: the latter means *showing respect*. *Respectable* may also mean *not inconsiderable* (*a respectable sum of money*) but even so it is probably wrongly used for *respectful* in

After being nearly knocked-out in the sixth round, he wisely began the seventh by keeping at a respectable distance.

respective, respectively. Fowler claims that 'of ten sentences in which they occur, nine would be improved by their removal', and that they are 'words seldom needed, but pretentious writers drag them in at every opportunity for the air of thoroughness and precision they are supposed to give to a sentence'.

Respective: properly pertaining to, or connected with, each individual, group, etc., of those in question.

An example of correct use:

Two new schools for boys and girls respectively are to be built to replace the existing four.

Without *respectively*, the sentence would have meant *Two mixed schools are to be built* ...

Wrong uses:

A communiqué will be issued simultaneously in Jerusalem and Cairo respectively.

Omit *respectively*, which adds nothing.

restive

> If the fire-bell rings, all workers must go immediately to
> their respective assembly-points.

This is better, though *own* would have sufficed, and both *respective*
and *own* are unnecessary in view of *their*.

> He has degrees from Manchester and Oxford
> respectively.

This is wrong use: omit *respectively*, and insert *both* before *Manchester*
if emphasis is required.

restive means *unmanageable, rejecting control* and does not mean the same
as *restless* (constantly stirring or active).

rethink as a verb (We must *rethink* our holiday plans = We must *think
again about* our holiday plans) has the merit of being slightly economical, but as a noun (We must *have a rethink about* our holiday plans)
it seldom has. New words justify their place in the language only if
they add a new shade of meaning or if they are markedly more economical than existing words or expressions. By these criteria, *rethink*
is superfluous.

retort is sharper than *reply*.

revenge, whether noun or verb, is best applied to the personal satisfac-
tion of an offence done to oneself:

> He will wish to take his revenge for his humiliation (*or*
> to revenge his humiliation) in last season's Final.

Avenge, and the corresponding noun *vengeance*, have to do with retri-
bution inflicted on behalf of someone else. That is to say, the avenger,
or the person seeking to exact vengeance, is motivated by a sense of
justice, not by personal resentment.

reversal is the act or process of turning in the opposite direction (*a
reversal of policy*). *Reversion*, apart from its legal meanings, is a return
to a previous state (*a reversion to his normal behaviour*). The correct word
for a set-back is *reverse*, not *reversal*.

reverse. See **reversal**.

reversion. See **reversal**.

revert back is ungrammatical, because *revert* means *go back, fall back,
turn back, return to former state*. The notion of *back* is contained in the
re of *revert* (as it is in *return*, *reverse*, etc.), and so the *back* in *revert back*
is superfluous. See **tautology**.

review means *survey*, and is not to be confused with *revue*, the only
meaning of which is theatrical.

126

revue. See **review**.

rhetorical question. A question to which no answer is expected. Often used as a device by public speakers, since asking questions is easier than making statements.

rise. See **raise**.

roof has the plural **roofs**.

route. The form *routeing* should be used, not *routing* which means *defeating*.

S

sadism is a form of perversion marked by love of cruelty. Not to be confused with **masochism**.

Saint (abbreviation *St*). See **St**.

same is sometimes wrongly used in such contexts as
He made the same speech that he made last week.
Either omit *same* (as being redundant) or say
He made the same speech as the one (that/which) he made last week.
Avoid *the same* as a pronoun in such cases as
I have received your letter and thank you for (the) same.
This is archaic, pretentious and unnecessary: the simple pronoun *it* (*them*, etc.) suffices.

sarcasm should not be confused with **irony**. *Sarcasm* is the use of bitter and wounding remarks in a direct fashion. Irony can be bitter, but it is indirect, and may be light-hearted. See **irony**.

saw (in the sense of *cut*) has *sawed* as past tense, and (usually) *sawn* as past participle.

scan: look intently at all parts successively of. It does NOT mean *look quickly or carelessly at*.

scarce and **rare** have similar meanings. The former means *not plentiful*, usually temporarily; the latter means *seldom found*, and is additionally associated with exceptional quality. Thus *potatoes are scarce this winter*, but *a rare book*.

scarcely is virtually a negative, and care should be taken not to use it with a second negative illogically.
I don't have scarcely any time.

127

scarcely ... than

and
>He had not enough time scarcely to unbuckle his safety-
>belt.

should be
>I scarcely have any time.
>He scarcely had enough time to unbuckle his safety-belt.

See **double negative**.

scarcely ... than should be *scarcely ... when* in such uses as
>Scarcely were the elections over *than* the first
>expressions of dissatisfaction were heard.

It is acceptable to use *scarcely ... before*, but never *scarcely ... than*.

sceptic. See **septic**.

schizophrenia is a mental disease; it is unnecessary, inaccurate and insensitive to use the word as a pretentious or jocular alternative to *indecisiveness*.

Scot(tish). See **Scotch**.

Scotch. The adjective *Scottish* (or *Scots*) and the noun *Scot* are preferred to *Scotch* except in such idioms as *Scotch whisky*, *Scotch tweeds* and a few others.

scotch, as a verb, means *wound without killing* (as in Macbeth's *We have scotched the snake, not killed it*). The use of the word to mean *kill* or *destroy* is widespread (scotch this rumour, proposal, suggestion, etc.) and wrong.

seasonable: suitable to the season (*seasonable weather* is that which is to be expected at a particular season). *Seasonal*: in season (*seasonal vegetables, seasonal employment* are to be found in certain seasons).

seasonal. See **seasonable**.

see where should be *see that* in such uses as
>Did you see where (*i.e.* read that *or* see on television that)
>the price of beer is going up next month?

seem is sometimes wrongly used, as in
>There doesn't seem to be anyone in.

which should be
>There seems not to be anyone in.

128

It is the 'being in' which is the negative, not the 'seeming', and *not* should be placed accordingly, close as possible to *to be*.

Similarly, *I can't seem to* should be *I seem unable to*.

seemed. There is sometimes confusion between *seemed to be* and *seem to have been*. The following are correct:

He seemed (*i.e. in the past*) to be worried.

He seems (i.e. *he seems to me now*) to have been worried.

(*in the past*)

There is no need for two past tenses, as in

He seemed to have been worried

unless the intended sense is

He seemed (*in the past*) to have been worried (*further in the past*).

semi-colon. The semi-colon (;) can only be used to link parts of a sentence that consist of main clauses (see **sentence 3**). It is stronger than a comma, weaker than a full stop, and is used within a sentence to join parts which are related by virtue of their subject matter, but which the writer does not wish to separate into individual sentences, perhaps because to do so would produce a jerky effect. In other words, a semi-colon can be used to join sentences if the writer wishes to run them together in the interests of smoothness or of a particular style he wishes to achieve.

He did not go to work on Monday morning; he was
feeling increasingly under the weather; there were times
when his head seemed to be spinning; worst of all,
thoughts which he had struggled for weeks to keep
under control were now threatening to plague him with
agonising intensity.

Note the following errors:

(a) *The head came off the hammer, it broke the glass.*

Two sentences cannot be joined by a comma. A semi-colon could have been used instead, because the two sentences are closely related. Alternatively, *and* could have been used as a linking word instead of the comma, or a full stop could have been put after *hammer*.

(b) *There was no arrogance in his nature; and he was always willing to listen to the opinions of others.*

Omit *and*: the semi-colon is a strong enough link without the assistance of a conjunction. Alternatively, replace the semi-colon by a comma, or start a new sentence: ... *in his nature. He was always* ...

sensual

(c) *Four car-parks are to be opened next year; a development which is long overdue.*

A semi-colon can only be used to link main clauses, i.e. groups of words which make complete sense on their own. The words after the semi-colon in this sentence do not constitute a main clause. A comma (or dash) should have been used here.

sensual: excessively inclined to the gratification of the senses (especially in sexual activities). *Sensuous* lacks the suggestion of condemnation which the use of *sensual* carries, and means *having to do with the senses; keenly alive to the pleasures of sensation.*

sensuous. See **sensual.**

sentence: a group of words which makes complete sense, forms a statement, question, command or exclamation, and contains a finite verb, i.e. a verb with a subject (see **verb 3**). A sentence must begin with a capital letter and end with a full stop, question mark or exclamation mark.

1. In its simplest form a sentence may contain only one finite verb:
    I *am* happy.

It is possible for a much longer sentence to contain only one finite verb:

Dover Castle, a magnificent example of Norman
architecture, overlooks the sea, providing a fine spectacle
for the thousands of tourists crossing the English
Channel every year.

The finite verb is *overlooks*, and its subject is *Dover Castle*. The other verbs (*providing, crossing*) are non-finite verbs. See **verb 5 (b)**.

2. In a command, the subject of the verb is usually suppressed.

Watch your step.

means

(You must) watch your step.

and so *watch* is a finite verb even though its subject is not stated. The same applies to all commands in which verbs are used in this way, so a command constitutes a full sentence. See also **interjection**.

3. (a) A sentence may consist of two clauses linked by a conjunction.

The frost was keen and the lake froze.

This statement could have been expressed as two separate and complete sentences

The frost was keen. The lake froze.

130

If they are joined together they become one sentence consisting of two clauses. Note that both clauses are capable of standing on their own, each making complete sense: neither is dependent on the other. They are called *main clauses*.

See **clause 1**.

Sometimes a sentence of this kind may be slightly compressed:

He shut the door and went out.

This means

He shut the door and he went out.

but the second *he* is dropped because repetition is unnecessary. The grammatical structure (main clause + main clause) remains unchanged, even though the subject of the second main clause has been omitted.

(b) Similarly, a sentence may consist of three or more main clauses:

The lights dimmed, the audience fell silent and the curtain rose.

Here the first two clauses are linked by a comma which does the work of a conjunction (e.g. *and*) and avoids needless repetition. The grammatical structure is still main clause + main clause + main clause.

The firework glowed. The firework burst into a shower of sparks. The firework spluttered. The firework went out.

These four separate sentences could be run into a single sentence of four main clauses by linking them with conjunctions:

The firework glowed and the firework burst into a shower of sparks and the firework sputtered and the firework went out.

Both these versions are obviously clumsy, repetitious, monotonous and ugly. It is clearly better to economise by omitting the repeated subject (*the firework*) and replacing some of the conjunctions with commas to do their linking work:

The firework glowed, burst into a shower of sparks, sputtered and went out.

Despite this compression, the sentence still consists of four main clauses (every verb is still finite even though its subject is not stated in every case: we know what it is) and the four clauses are properly linked. Note that a linking comma is not needed before *and* because this conjunction can do the linking work on its own. It would not have been wrong to have

131

inserted a comma there, however, if a pause would have been helpful to the sense or the style.

See **comma 8.**

4. All the sentences so far described have consisted of main clauses, i.e. groups of words containing finite verbs and capable of making complete sense on their own. In the sentence

The vacuum cleaner, which we bought only last week, already needs repair.

there are two finite verbs: *bought,* of which the subject is *we*; and *needs,* of which the subject is *vacuum cleaner.* There are therefore two clauses in the sentence:

1. The vacuum cleaner already needs repair
2. which we bought only last week.

The first of these makes sense on its own, and is the main clause or main statement of the sentence: it is what the whole sentence is about. The second does not make complete sense on its own; it is a subordinate part of the sentence (describing *vacuum cleaner* in the main clause) and cannot function or have any significance without the main clause, on which it depends for its sense and meaning.

A sentence can therefore consist of a main clause and a subordinate clause (see **clause 1** and **2** for several other examples). It can also consist of several main clauses and subordinate clauses. It can have main clauses without subordinate clauses, as we have seen, but subordinate clauses cannot, by definition, exist without main clauses. Here is an example of a sentence containing two main clauses (italicised) and two subordinate clauses:

As the bus moved on, *a little boy in a school blazer paused beside the vacant seat* and *then moved up the aisle in deference to a smartly-dressed woman* who followed behind, carrying a large shopping-bag and a poodle.

The first subordinate clause is

As the bus moved on

which describes when the verb in the main clause (*paused*) happened. The second subordinate clause is

who followed behind

which is an adjectival clause describing *woman.* The final words

carrying a large shopping-bag and a poodle,

are not a clause because the verb (*carrying*) does not have a subject; they are an adjectival phrase describing *woman.*

See **clause** and **verb**.

separate is frequently mis-spelt. Note also *separable, inseparable, separation*, etc.

septic (the medical word, as distinct from *sceptic*, pronounced *skeptic*, meaning *doubter*) is spelt as pronounced, despite *sceptre, scene*, etc.

service, as a verb, means *repair, overhaul* or *maintain*. It is used as an unnecessary alternative to *serve* in

> The new roads that service the recently completed
> housing estate ...

sew has *sewed* or *sewn* as past participles.

shall, will. (These are complex words, and it is impossible to summarise all their uses concisely: fuller explanations are to be found in any good dictionary. The following points deal with the main problems; minor ones are ignored in view of the fact that both words are nowadays used interchangeably.)

1. To express the future, use *shall* in the first person singular (*I shall*) and first person plural (*we shall*), and *will* in all other cases. This is a fundamental rule, though Scots will disagree.

2. *Will* (including *I will* and *we will*) is used to express willingness, resolve, wish, determination, intention:

> I will come, whatever the difficulties.

It is also possible to use *will* to express a command:

> You will do as you are told.

3. *Shall* is used to express obligation, necessity or permission:

> Shall I (=ought I to) wrap it up?

It is also used in clauses introduced by *that* after verbs expressing desire, intention, demand, etc.

> It is intended that the work shall be finished before
> summer.

4. Some grammar books say: to express the future, use *will* with *I* and *we*, and *shall* in all other cases; to express willingness or obligation, reverse the rule (i.e. use *shall* with *I* and *we*, and *will* in all other cases).

should, would. (See note at beginning of **shall, will**.)

1. *Should* is a tense of *shall* in its sense of *be obliged to*. *Would* is a tense of *will* in its sense of *wish, resolve, be determined to*.

> See **shall, will 2, 3.**
>> I *should have* done it. (I ought to have done it)
>> I *wouldn't* do it. (I did not wish to do it)
>> I *would* point out that ... (I wish to point out that ...)

should like

2. In other uses, as parts of verbs rather than as verbs with their own meanings, use *should* with *I* and *we*, and *would* in all other cases. (This corresponds with the rule stated under **shall, will 1**.)
> I should be grateful if you would ...
> It would be convenient ...
> We should prefer to wait.

An important exception to this rule is that in many subordinate clauses introduced by *that*, *should* is used in all cases, never *would*:
> It is unfortunate that he *should* be offended.

See also **to have, subjunctive**.

should like is correct in
> I should like to have been there.

The common
> I should have liked to have been there.

is not: one past tense (*should have liked*) is sufficient without putting the infinitive into the past as well. Thus
> I should have liked to be there.

show has the past participle *shown*; the alternative *showed* is best avoided.

similar is followed by *to*, not *as*, and is wrongly used in
> The Union is determined not to make a similar mistake, in failing to gain public support, as the air-traffic controllers.

which should be
> ... make a mistake similar to *that of* the air-traffic controllers in failing to gain ...

Note that *similar* does not mean the same as *same*: the former has to do with likeness, the latter with identity.
> See **similarly**.

similarly is the adverb formed from the adjective *similar*.
> Their reasons were similar.

is correct: so is
> Other parts of the country are similarly affected.

It is an error to use *similar* when *similarly* is needed, as in
> Since the war, the German economy has not developed similar to the British economy.

The adverbial form *similarly* is needed because the word describes a verb, *developed*. This sentence could also be corrected
> ... has not developed in a way similar to that of the ...

simile. See **metaphor**.

simplistic is sometimes used as a substitute for *simple* by those who assume that longer words are always better. In fact, it has to do with an archaic use of *simple* as a noun meaning either a medicine of only one constituent, usually herbal, or a herb or plant used for medical purposes. A *simplist* was a herbalist, and *simplistic* the corresponding adjective. Nowadays, to describe someone's opinions as *simplistic* is to denote naivety, lack of sophistication or even stupidity.

singular 1. If a noun or pronoun names a single person or thing it is said to be (*in the*) *singular*. If it names more than one person or thing, it is said to be (*in the*) *plural*. Examples:

Singular	Plural	Singular	Plural
potato	potatoes	I	we
loaf	loaves	he, she, it	they
ally	allies	you	you
man	men	experience	experiences
sheep	sheep	child	children

The general rule in English is that the plural of nouns is formed by adding *s* to the singular (*house, houses*). The following are the main exceptions to this rule:

(*a*) singular nouns ending in *s, ch, sh, x, z* and *o* add *es*:
brush, brushes; pitch, pitches; fox, foxes; tomato, tomatoes.

(*b*) singular nouns ending in *f* or *fe* change the *f* or *fe* into *ves*:
wife, wives; life, lives; half, halves.
Exceptions: *chief, chiefs; proof, proofs; roof, gulf, dwarf.*

(*c*) singular nouns ending in *consonant+y* change the *y* into *i* and add *es*:
country, countries; diary, diaries; fly, flies.
But *vowel +y* follows the general rule: *boy, boys; toy, toys.*

(*d*) several nouns have irregular plurals: *child, children; man, men; foot, feet; mouse, mice; goose, geese; tooth, teeth.*

(*e*) some nouns do not change in the plural: *cod, deer, salmon, sheep, trout.*

(*f*) some nouns have no singular: *scissors, billiards, dregs, measles.*

This list is far from exhaustive, and there are special problems with foreign words which have entered the language. However, a good dictionary will normally indicate irregular plurals.

2. Some verbs have different singular and plural forms:
he *is*, they *are*; the village *lies*, the villages *lie*.
The rule is that if the subject of the verb is singular, the verb must be singular; if the subject is plural, so must the verb be:
The car is in need of repair. *The cars are* waiting.

See **each, either ... or, everyone, noun 2, there is**.

3. If two or more singular words are joined by conjunctions, they become plural and take a plural verb:

> Settlement of the strike and a return to work *are* expected this week.

> We turned the corner and there *were* John and Mary.

Note that *with* is not a conjunction, so

> A man *with* a herd of cows *is* holding up the traffic.

but A man *and* a herd of cows *are* holding up the traffic.

A few common expressions (bread and butter, fish and chips, bacon and eggs, salt and pepper, whisky and soda) may be regarded as singular entities because of the very close connexion between their two parts.

4. Some plural nouns (e.g. scissors, trousers, gloves) are often used with *a pair of*. The expression then becomes singular:

> There *is* a pair of slippers under the sofa.

Compasses (the drawing instrument) should always be *a pair of compasses*.

See **one**.

5. Some plural nouns may be used with singular verbs when the emphasis is on the single entity denoted by the noun:

> Ten years *is* a long time.

> The United Nations *has* decided ...

See **noun 2, pronoun 8 (b)**.

6. Errors sometimes occur in long sentences:

> This must be the most hilarious, the most disappointing, the most trivial and the most penetrating political memoirs ever published.

The writer began this sentence thinking of something singular (*This*), presumably a book. By the time he got to the end of his long sentence, the book had been changed to the plural *memoirs*. *This* should therefore have been changed to *these* (or *memoirs* changed to the singular *collection of memoirs*).

situation. Perhaps nowadays the most over-used word in the English language. Its sudden popularity is much to be deplored, and its use usually signifies a lazy avoidance of a more accurate word, or an attempt to add supposed style. More usually still, it is totally unnecessary. Of many examples which could be quoted, the most recent to assault the ears occurred in a television interview with a motorway policeman who referred to 'a fog situation': he meant 'fog'.

size is often used wrongly in place of *sized* in such adjectival compounds as *medium-sized, fair-sized,* etc. See **large-size**.

skilful is often mis-spelt with double l in the middle. Note *skilfully.*

slander and **slanderous** refer to spoken defamatory statements. See **libel**.

slang is language of a highly colloquial type, considered as below the level of standard educated speech, and consisting either of new words or of current words employed in some special sense (*Shorter Oxford English Dictionary*). It excludes **jargon** and dialect words, which are not current enough generally to justify being called slang. If a slang word achieves greater respectability, it passes into colloquialism, and may even reach Standard English. Slang has no place in formal writing or speaking, but the ever-increasing informality of modern times makes it difficult to lay down clearer guidance.

slippy, for slippery, is described as 'vulgar' by the *C.O.D.*, and is also found in slang. It should be avoided.

smelled is not incorrect, but *smelt* is more usual both as past tense and past participle of *smell.*

so that (in the sense *in order that*) should not be shortened to *so.*
> They worked quickly, so they could leave early.
does not make clear which of two possible shades of meaning is intended:
> They worked quickly, so (that) they could leave early.
> They worked quickly, (and) so they could leave early.
The difference is that between purpose and consequence.
It is wrong to use *so as* for *so that* (in order that) in
> They worked quickly so as they could leave early.

sociable, social. The former has to do with companionship, the latter with the community. *Sociable*: friendly, enjoying the company of others. *Social*: concerned with society (*social contract, social problem*) or with mutual relations in society (*social club, social worker*).

some place (else) is an American expression: the normal English is *somewhere (else)*.

somebody and **someone** are singular words, and care should be taken to ensure that any verb they govern, or any pronoun referring back to them, is likewise singular. See **everybody**.

sort. *Those/these sort of* is common and incorrect, as in
> Those sort of people are always helpful.

sort of

The singular noun *sort* needs a singular *that/this* and a singular verb:
That sort of people is ...
Alternatively (but more clumsy and less accurate)
Those sorts of people are ...
See **adjective 5**.

sort of is often used as a meaningless addition to a sentence
I sort of dropped it.
or as a substitute for *rather, to some extent*:
You sort of promised.
The former should be avoided because it is nonsensical; the latter is colloquial.

sound like. See **like 1**.

sound out, in the sense *enquire into the opinions of*, means no more than *sound*, and the unnecessary *out* should not be used.

sparing of, not *sparing with*.

speciality, specialty. The words have identical meanings, but the former is more commonly used.

spectrum. There is little or no justification for using this word as a colourful substitute for the perfectly adequate *range* in
Schools which deal with the whole spectrum of ability ...
The West End caters for the whole spectrum of theatrical tastes.

speech marks. See **quotation marks**.

speed has *sped* as past tense and past participle; but *speed up*, and *speed* in the sense of *drive fast*, have *speeded*.

spell may have either *spelled* or *spelt* as past participle and past tense, but *spelt* is the more common.

spelling. There are many spelling-rules (such as 'i before e except after c, whenever the sound you are making is ee') and many exceptions to most of them. The simplest and best rule is to use a dictionary and learn by heart any words which are commonly mis-spelt.

spill may have either *spilled* or *spilt* as past tense and past participle.

split infinitive. See **verb 5 (a)**.

spoil may have *spoiled* or *spoilt* as past tense and past participle (except when the verb means *plunder*, in which case only *spoiled* is permitted).

138

spoonful: quantity that fills a spoon. The plural is *spoonfuls*.
See **handful**.

St. Those writers who recommend that abbreviations which have the
first and last letters of the full word (e.g. *Mr, Mrs, Dr*) do not need
a full stop would argue that *St* is the correct abbreviation of *Saint*.
It is best to retain *St.* to mean *Street*.

stadium has the plural *stadia*, but like many words of foreign derivation
it nowadays often has the more English plural *stadiums*.

Standard English is that form of the English language which is spoken
by the generality of cultured people in Great Britain (*Shorter Oxford
English Dictionary*). It excludes dialect and slang. Colloquialism is informal Standard English, and consists of a vocabulary and, occasionally, a syntax (and even a pronunciation, e.g. *I'll* for *I will*) which
are appropriate to familiar conversation, not to formal or dignified
contexts. Colloquialisms, in time, may be promoted to the status of
Standard English or demoted to that of slang. Language is alive and
constantly changing, and movement among all its areas is always taking place. Dictionaries record the status of words and their grammar
as they exist at the time of publication, and are the most reliable sources
of information about Standard English.

standpoint is often used unnecessarily, meaninglessly or clumsily:
> From the welfare standpoint, the tax changes are to be
> welcomed.

is intended to mean *From the standpoint of those concerned with welfare* ... Other clearer variants: *As far as welfare is concerned* ...; *In their
effect on welfare,* ...

start up. The *up* should be omitted if it adds nothing to the meaning
of the verb.

stationary, stationery. It is easy to remember that the *-ary* version is
the adjective (*a* for adjective) meaning *not moving*, and the other one
is therefore the noun meaning *writing materials*.

stigma. The plural is *stigmas*. The alternative plural *stigmata* is reserved
to denote the marks resembling the wounds on the crucified body
of Christ and said to be impressed on the bodies of certain saints and
other devout persons (*Shorter Oxford English Dictionary*).

stimulant, stimulus. Both stimulate, but the former is usually medical,
meaning *something which produces an increase of vital energy*. Alcohol
and coffee are stimulants. *Stimulus* is generally non-medical, and

means *that which rouses to activity or energy*: a pupil usually responds to the *stimulus* of good teaching. The plural of *stimulus* is *stimuli*, the final *-i* pronounced *eye* or *ee*: the former is correct, the latter more common.

stop off, stop over are Americanisms which have established themselves firmly. *Stop off* means no more than *stop*, and the redundant *off* should be avoided. *Stop over* is slightly more useful, but if *over* means *overnight*, as it usually does, why not say so? *Make a stop-over at* is long-winded and ugly for *stay (overnight) at*.

storey (plural *storeys*): any of the parts into which a building is divided horizontally. *Story* (plural *stories*) is not incorrect in this sense, but is best reserved for *piece of narrative*. Both *three-storeyed* and *three-storied* are correct, but the former is preferable.

strait, straight. The former means *narrow, limited, confined*, as in strait jacket, straitened circumstances, the strait and narrow, the Straits of Dover. *Straight* means *without curve or bend*.

strata is the plural of *stratum* and must not be used if it were singular, as it is used in *a different strata of society*.

strategy is not the same as *tactics*. The former, meaning *generalship, management* (of a campaign), *art* (of warfare, etc), is abstract; *tactics* are devices and procedures used in carrying out a strategy. The distinction is useful and deserves to be retained.

stratum. See **strata**.

subject. The subject of a sentence or clause is the word or group of words that performs the action of the verb. The subjects of the verbs in the following sentences are italicised:

> *Matthew Arnold* once said that the *secret of style* was to
> have something to say and to say it as clearly as *you* can.
> *This* is over-simple, but *it* will do well enough as a first
> principle for the kind of writing in which *emotional
> appeal* plays no part. *The most prevalent disease in present-
> day writing* is a tendency to say what *one* has to say in as
> complicated a way as possible. Instead of being simple,
> terse and direct, *it* is stilted, long-winded and
> circumlocutory.
>
> (Gowers, *The Complete Plain Words*)

To locate the subject, find the verb and ask: who or what is performing the action described in this verb?

A singular subject needs a singular verb: a plural subject needs a plural verb. Breaches of this rule are common when a writer fails to think clearly about what precisely is the subject:

> Further information about our low-budget holidays and charter flights, together with full details of booking arrangements, are available from local offices.

The verb in this sentence is *are*. What is it that *are* available? The answer is *information*, which is singular. Thus *are* should be *is*. Having placed a singular subject at the beginning of his sentence, the writer goes on at some length, using a number of plural words (holidays, flights, details, arrangements), and by the time he reaches his verb it has been attracted ungrammatically into the plural.

Note that a singular verb is necessary if its subject is *either, neither, more than one* or *each*. See also **either ... or, neither ... nor, none, singular** and **there is**.

subjunctive. One of the four **moods** of verbs, i.e. one of the classes of verb-functions. The function of the subjunctive mood is to indicate a wish, a condition or a purpose; the subjunctive normally occurs in sentences containing *if* and *that*.

Many people use the subjunctive instinctively (*I should like to go*) without realising that there is anything noteworthy about it. Such common uses of the subjunctive are not dealt with here, because they present no problems.

Most verbs in the subjunctive are not immediately recognisable, because their form is the same as in other uses. Those changes in verb-form that do occur in the subjunctive are described in **5** below.

The main difficulties are with the verb *to be*, and especially with *were*. The following illustrations concentrate on *were*.

1. The subjunctive is found in some subordinate clauses introduced by *that* in sentences expressing desire, wish, will or request, sometimes in formal language

> I propose that he *be* asked ...

sometimes in less elevated language

> I wish that it *were* over and done with.

Note that *that* may be omitted and 'understood':

> I wish you *were* here.

The *were* of the last illustration looks like the past tense of *is*. It is, however, the past subjunctive, which can refer to the present or the future. As one grammarian (Gowers/Fraser) has written, 'What looks like the past tense does not denote pastness; it denotes a greater call on the imagination.' See **5 (b)** below.

141

2. The subjunctive is also found in sentences containing *if* clauses when such clauses do not state fact.

> If he *were* here (i.e. but he isn't), he *would be* able to help.

Note the difference between this subjunctive mood and the normal indicative mood:

> If he *is* here, he *will be* able to help.

Sometimes the *if* clause is disguised:

> *Were* he here (i.e. if he *were* here), he would be able to help.

This rule only applies when an *if* clause contains *were*.

3. The subjunctive is found after *as if* and *as though* if the following clause is NOT accepted as true:

> He spoke to me as if I *were* a complete idiot.

4. The subjunctive occurs in some common phrases, usually expressing a wish or request that something may occur:

> God *help* us. (i.e. not *helps*)
> *Be* that as it may. (i.e. not *Is*)
> *Come* what may.
> If need *be*.
> Far *be* (not *is*) it from me to ...
> So *be* it. (not *is*)

Note how the form of the subjunctive differs from the indicative (in brackets).

5. The subjunctive is only found as a separate verb-form in

(*a*) the present tense of *to be*, in which the subjunctive is:

> I be, you be, he/she/it be, we be, they be.
> She insisted that she be allowed to take part.

(*b*) the past tense of *to be*, in which *were* is used with all persons:

> I were, he/she/it were, etc.
> What if she were to refuse?

(*c*) the present tense of other verbs, in which only the third person singular (he, she, it) changes. It does so by taking the same verb-form as the present tense plural. Thus

> It is essential that he *stop*. (not *stops*, which is the normal present-tense singular)
> We suggested that he *have* (not *has*) leave of absence.

In the present tense, one would say *he stops, he has*, which have the plural forms *they stop, they have*. In the subjunctive, the *he* (and *she*, *it*) takes the plural form of the present tense: *he stop, he have*.

These examples are in accordance with the facts set out in

paragraph 1 above, but the use of the straightforward present tense

> It is essential that he *stops*.
> We suggested that he *has* leave of absence.

would not be regarded as incorrect nowadays.

subordinate clause. See **clause**.

subsequent: following. *Consequent*: resulting. Do not use *subsequent to* if *after* or *following* suffices: the simpler expression is normally preferable.

See **consequent (up)on**.

subsidence. The word is pronounced with the emphasis on the first syllable or the second (as in *side*). The former is preferable.

subsidiary is sometimes mis-spelt *subsiduary* or *subsidary*.

substantial is often pretentious for *large*.

substitute: make (a person or thing) fill a place or discharge a function *for* another. It does NOT mean *replace* (person or thing) *by* or *with* another. Football commentators are particularly guilty of claiming 'X has been substituted by Y' when they mean 'The manager has substituted Y *for* X' or 'Y has been substituted *for* X' or 'X has been *replaced by* Y.' In other words, one substitutes *for*, not *by* or *with*, and one does not use *substitute* when *replace* is needed.

such, when used as an adjective or pronoun, should be followed by *as*. The following is incorrect:

> Prizes will be given to such of the competitors *who* complete the course in less than an hour.

This should read either

> ... to those competitors who ...

or

> ... to such (of the) competitors *as* complete the course ...

suffix: letter or syllable added to the end of a word to change its meaning. Some examples:

Suffix	Meaning	Example
-isation	making	standardisation
-ful	full of	beautiful, handful

Other common suffixes include *-able*, *-ible* (able to), *-fy* (make), *-ise* (make), *-less* (lacking), *-ous* (having the quality of).

summarisation (meaning *summary*) is the daftest, most pompous and least defensible example of the abuse described at **containerise**.

superfluous is pronounced with the emphasis on the second syllable, not the third.

superior means *higher* (in position, rank, quality, etc.), and thus it is as ungrammatical to say *more superior* as it would be to say *more higher*.
    Superior to is correct, not *superior than*.

superlative degree. See **adjective 2, adverb 2**.

supernumerary is spelt and pronounced so.

supersede, not *supercede*.

supine. See **prone**.

surprised is often used in such expressions as
        I shouldn't be surprised if it didn't rain.
when the opposite meaning is intended, i.e. either
        I shouldn't be surprised if it *did* rain.
or
        I should be surprised if it didn't rain.

syllable. The basic unit of pronunciation, consisting of a **vowel** or vowel-sound with, usually, a consonant or consonants before it, or after it, or both before and after. The word *luminous* has three syllables, *lum-in-ous* (the last syllable contains two vowels but they are pronounced as one and make a single vowel-sound). A word consisting of a single syllable is called a monosyllable, e.g. *yacht, scythe* (*y*=vowel-sound; *e*=unsounded), *please*.

syndrome is a medical term meaning a set of symptoms which occur together, suggesting an illness. The word may also be used metaphorically to denote something non-medical: one can speak, light-heartedly perhaps, of a motor-cycle syndrome discernible in young people who incessantly talk and read about motor-cycles, ride them, tinker with them, and adopt a distinctive dress, language, way of life and set of moral standards. But it should always be remembered that a syndrome is a coming together of several *symptoms*; it is not a disease. Neither a symptom nor a syndrome can be *suffered*, though both can be expressed, exhibited, presented, observed, etc.

Like many fashionable metaphors, therefore, *syndrome* should be used with care, lest the user betray his ignorance.

synonym. A word which means the same as another. *Lazy* and *indolent* are synonyms. The opposite of synonym is **antonym**.

syntax. The rules governing sentence construction.

T

take it easy. See **easier**.

target. A target is something one aims to hit. It is a misuse of the word to define success in terms of 'reaching', 'attaining' or 'exceeding' a target.

tautology is unintended or unnecessary repetition. Repetition for the sake of emphasis is a permitted feature of style, but tautology is a fault of grammar.

For example, *new innovation* is tautological: the *new* is redundant because *innovation* means, by definition, something new, the introduction of novelty. *Mutual cooperation*, beloved of politicians, is tautological because the notion of mutuality is contained in the meaning of *cooperation*, the *co-* part of which means *together*. Both *new* and *mutual*, therefore, add nothing which is not already contained in the meanings of the two nouns.

Other common examples of tautology include *adequate enough*, *assemble together*, *close proximity*, *combine together*, *final upshot*, *blend* or *collect together*, *necessary requisite*, *past history*, *protrude out*, *renew again*, *revert back*, *sink down*, *unfilled vacancy*.
See also **again**, **back**, **equally as**, **together**.

(*C.O.D.* defines tautology as 'saying of the same thing twice over in different words'. Partridge lists *twice over* as an example of tautology!)

tendentious does not mean *biased* but *having an underlying purpose, calculated to advance a cause*. A speech or piece of writing can be properly said to be tendentious if it advances an argument either explicit or implied.

tense. See **verb 2**.

terms. See **regard**.

than

than must be used with care. The two sentences
> He is taller than me.
> He is taller than I.

are both acceptable (though the first is slightly colloquial). In the first, *than* is being used as a preposition, and is therefore followed by the accusative *me* (see **preposition**). In the second, *than* is being used as a conjunction, introducing the clause *than I (am)*, though the *am* is not stated in accordance with common practice:
> Will you do it, or shall I? (i.e. or shall I *do it*?)

There may be occasions, however, when this dual use of *than* may create ambiguity:
> You like her better than me.

means
> You like her better than (you like) me.

or
> You like her better than I do.

In such cases it is necessary to spell out the sentences in full.

Adverbs and adjectives in the comparative degree (see **adjective 1**, **adverb 2**) may be followed by *than*, but the only other words that can be used with *than* are *other, otherwise, else* and *elsewhere*. The following are therefore incorrect:
> More than three times as many people came *than* had been expected. (*than* should be *as*)
> He prefers riding his bicycle to work *than* driving. (*than* should be *to*)

See also **different from, inferior to, superior** for other wrong uses of *than*.

Note that *than whom* is always correct, never *than who*.

thankfully means *gratefully, full of thanks*:
> He took their advice thankfully.

Accordingly,
> Thankfully, he died quickly.

means that he died full of thanks: he may well have done, but it is more likely that the writer intended the meaning
> I am thankful that he died quickly.

There is no good reason for stretching the meaning of *thankfully* in this way, and this use should be avoided. See also **hopefully**.

that may be used instead of *who* or *which* when introducing subordinate clauses which define rather than merely describe. Compare these sentences:

146

I dislike trains that are dirty.

I dislike trains, which are dirty.

The first sentence means that I dislike only dirty trains, and implies that otherwise I enjoy rail travel. The second means that I dislike *all* trains, and gives a reason. The first is an example of a sentence with a defining clause; the second has a describing one. A defining clause is so integral that, if it were omitted, the sense would be very seriously incomplete, misleading or unhelpful. If the defining clause is removed from the first sentence, the basic sense changes importantly from *I dislike some trains* to *I dislike all trains*; if the describing clause is removed from the second sentence, the basic sense (*I dislike all trains*) remains intact. A describing clause is normally introduced by a comma. A defining clause is essential, cannot be put within commas (the clause is so integral that no pause separates it from the rest of the sentence), and cannot be omitted without removing or significantly limiting the sense of the sentence. Defining clauses are best introduced by *that*.

Other examples:

The visitors that come at Easter are always elderly.

The visitors, who come at Easter, are always elderly.

The first implies that there are other visitors, at other seasons, and that they are not elderly. The second implies that visitors come only at Easter and are always elderly.

Send it to the office that deals with refunds.

Send it to the office, which deals with refunds.

The first implies that there are other offices, that these do not deal with refunds, and that *it* should be sent to the-office-that-deals-with-refunds. The second implies that there is only one office, and adds a helpful piece of description.

The use of *that* to introduce defining clauses is not obligatory (despite what some have written) though it is a nice point of grammar and careful writers will want to take advantage of it. The second sentences in all the above pairs could be rewritten without commas and would then mean the same as the first sentences. In other words

(*a*) *who* and *which* may be used to introduce defining clauses (as well as describing clauses) but good English prefers *that*.

(*b*) *that* can be used only to introduce defining clauses.

(*c*) defining clauses must not be marked off with commas.

See **adjective 5, comma 2, in order that**.

the. See **definite article**.

their is a possessive pronoun meaning *of them*. In all other cases, use *there*.

theirs

Note a possible confusion with *they're*, the abbreviated form of *they are*.

theirs is never spelt *their's*. See **pronoun 3**.

theirselves does not exist.

there. See **their**.

there is, there are cause no problems in simple sentences: the rule is that *there is* is used when referring to something singular:

There is an interesting broadcast at 9.30.

and *there are* when referring to something plural:

There are few worth buying.

Errors sometimes occur as sentences become longer:

There is your Uncle John to write to, and your grandparents.

This should have *are* because what is being referred to (Uncle John ... and your grandparents) is plural.

Another example of misuse comes from a *New Statesman* theatre review:

There's lively dialogue, wit and intelligence.

therefore is sometimes written with commas before and after it, and sometimes not. Usually, commas are unnecessary; if used, they have the effect of emphasising the preceding word. Note the difference in emphasis between

The sentences can therefore be expected to be severe.

and

The sentences can, therefore, be expected to be severe.

these. See **adjective 5**.

these kind of and similar expressions (*those sort of, these type of*) are slip-shod: a singular noun needs a singular *this* or *that*:

That kind of flower is ...

not

Those kind of flowers are ...

thing is a much over-used word, for which a more precise substitute can invariably be found.

this. See **adjective 5**.

those. See **adjective 5**.

through in the sense *because of* must be used carefully to avoid the sort of ambiguity found in a mother's letter to school:

I kept Frank at home yesterday because he had
diarrhoea through a hole in his shoe.

till. See **until**.

to. Users of English instinctively put a personal pronoun into the
accusative after the preposition *to*

It seems to *me* that ...

but are curiously prone to error when more than one personal
pronoun is to be used, e.g.

It may seem to you or I ... (where *I* must be *me*).

For the difference between *to* and *too*, see **too**.

to all intents and purposes. The last two words are superfluous.

to have. The perfect (or past) infinitive (e.g. *to have been, to have
done, to have seen*, etc.) is often used after *would have* and *should
have*

I should have liked to have been there

and after *had*

I had planned to have finished yesterday.

If the verb is in the past, there is no need to repeat the 'past-ness'
by putting the infinitive also into the past. The correct version of
the above sentence is

I should have liked to be there.

I had planned to finish yesterday.

See **should, would**.

together is unnecessary in *attach together, collaborate together, connect
together, gather together, join together, link together, meet together,
mingle together, mix together, unite together* and in all other cases
when a verb can express the notion of togetherness without the
assistance of *together*.

See **tautology**.

tolerant of, not *tolerant to*.

too is an adverb, used either with an adjective (*too fat*) or another adverb
(*too frequently*) to mean *excessively*, or used on its own to mean *also*
(*He grows roses too*). In all other cases, use *to*, which is never an adverb
except in *to and fro* and in the expressions *heave to, come to, bring to*.

trade union has as its plural *trade unions* (but note *Trades Union
Congress*).

tragic. See **journalese**.

transitive verb. See **verb 4**.

transpire does not mean *happen*, despite its frequent use in this sense, but *come to be known*.

transportation is an unnecessary word, meaning no more than *transport*.

trauma is used in medicine to describe deep shock produced by an injury, and in psychology to describe deep emotional shock. It is a weakening of English to use the word to describe any mildly alarming or upsetting feeling.

The *au* of trauma and *traumatic* is pronounced *or*.

truism does not mean *true thing*, but *self-evident or indisputable truth* or *hackneyed truth*.

try and followed by a verb (*try and open it*) is colloquial. The correct expression is *try to*, but *try and* is permitted if the intention is to encourage: *try and solve it yourself* implies that the effort will succeed (*try and you will solve it*).

type is a singular noun and needs the singular *this* or *that*.
> The management is familiar with these type of complaints.
should read *this type* (or *these types*) *of complaint*.

U

ultimate end, in the is an illiterate expression, because all ends are ultimate by definition. See **tautology**.

ultimatum may have *ultimatums* or *ultimata* in the plural. The former is the more usual.

underlining a word when writing is equivalent to using italics in print. The device should be used as rarely as possible, otherwise it loses the intended effect, which is to add special emphasis.

undiscriminating. See **indiscriminate**.

undoubtably does not exist, and is a confusion between *undoubtedly* and *indubitably*, both of which mean *certainly*.

undue, like *unduly*, should be used with care. It means *going beyond what is appropriate*.

150

> There is no cause for undue alarm.

means, as Gowers points out,

> There is no cause for alarm for which there is no cause.

which seems hardly worth saying. *Undue* and *unduly* are too often used when they add nothing (except nonsense) to the meaning of a sentence.

uneatable. See **inedible**.

unequal to, not *unequal for*.

unexceptionable, unexceptional. The former means *perfectly satisfactory or adequate*; *to whom or to which no exception can be taken*. The latter is the opposite of *exceptional*.

uninterested means *lacking in curiosity, concern or interest*. For general purposes it may be regarded as the opposite of *interested*. *Disinterested* has a quite different meaning: *impartial, unbiased*. See **disinterest** and **disinterested**, which are often incorrectly used in contexts which require *lack of interest* and *uninterested*.

unique. A much abused word. It means *single, sole, one and only, unparalleled, unrivalled, having no like or equal* (Shorter Oxford English Dictionary). Something unique is the only one of its kind, and there can be no shades of uniqueness. It is therefore nonsense to call something *rather unique*, or to attach to *unique* such words as *more, most, very, somewhat, comparatively*, because these words express degrees, and *unique* is an absolute. The following, from a television commentary, is typical of many abuses:

> The most unique feature of the house is its movable
> walls.

The error is to assume that *unique* means *rare, exceptional*, etc. It is quite in order to describe something as *very rare* or *quite exceptional*, but not to describe it as *very* or *quite unique*.

It is, however, permissible to say that something is *almost* or *nearly* unique. This means that something is not unique (so there is no question of degrees of uniqueness, to which objection has already been raised) but that it is one of a very small number of things.

unless and until is occasionally found. Use either *unless* or *until* but not both, because they have the same force. See **if and when**.

unreadable. See **illegible**.

unrepairable. See **repairable**.

until is often mis-spelt *untill*, presumably because of *till*.

151

until such time as

until such time as is unnecessarily long-winded for *until*.

up to date is so written except when it is used adjectivally, in which cases hyphens are necessary. Thus
> Bring me up to date.

but
> The book provides an up-to-date account.

up until is to be avoided: *until* alone is enough.

upward(s). The adjective is *upward* (*an upward glance*); the adverb may be either *upward* or *upwards*.

upward movement (of prices, unemployment figures, etc.) is some-times used by politicians and others who must feel that short words such as *rise* or *increase* are too painful.

urban, urbane. The former means *belonging to or characteristic of a city* (*urban decay, urban population*) and should not be confused with *urbane*, meaning *courteous, refined*.

usage does not mean the same as *use*. Usage is the *manner* of using (*With careful usage it will last several years*), or customary practice (see next paragraph). *Use* is the *act* of using (*It will be put to good use*).

Applied to language, *usage* is the way in which words are used. There are many ways, some of them described in this book, in which people's usage differs from the rules of grammar, but ultimately it is usage, not grammar, that determines the nature of English. Usage may be criticised, condemned and resisted; it may, in the course of time, be changed as a result of such criticism; but in the last resort, dictionaries and grammar books have to record what is, not what ought to be. What is standard practice in a language is governed by what is habitual, i.e. by usage.

use. See **usage**.

used to. The opposite of *I used to* (etc.) is *I used not to*, not *I didn't use to*. The verb *used* means *was/were accustomed*; if one wishes to express the negative of
> I used to ride a bicycle

it is necessary to ask which of the two verbs (*used, ride*) is to be nega-tived. Was it the custom (*used*) which did not take place, or was it the cycling (*ride*)? The answer is, the latter, and the *not* must therefore be placed before *ride*, not before *used*:
> I used *not to ride* a bicycle.

This is, however, a fine distinction in grammar, and the more common *didn't use to* would probably be regarded as acceptable, if still rather colloquial.

utilise, utilisation are excellent examples of a modern tendency to use at least three syllables when one will do. There are no circumstances (unless one wishes to be pompous) when these words are better than *use*.

V

various means *different, diverse,* NOT *certain* or *several.* The expression *various different,* as in
> The new Common Market regulations will have various different effects

is wrong, because *various* and *different* mean exactly the same thing. The sentence should have *several different* or simply *various* in place of *various different.*

've, the abbreviation of *have,* in *should've, can've, will've,* etc., often tricks children into writing *should of, can of,* etc., which are of course wrong.

vengeance. See **revenge**.

verb 1. The grammatical term to denote a word that states what someone or something does or is.

In its simplest form, a verb may be a single word (Time *flies;* I *will* not; *Did* she?), but often a verb consists of several words (I *have* recently *been* told; He *will* certainly not *agree*).

2. A verb may indicate past, present or future time, and its form will undergo change accordingly. (This change is called *inflexion*.) The different forms used for this purpose are called *tenses*. Some examples:

Present tense	Past tense	Future tense
I am	I was	I shall be
You see	You saw	You will see
He drives	He drove	He will drive
They dance	They danced	They will dance

Tenses may also indicate whether an action is, was or will be continuous or completed; if the latter, the verb is in the *perfect* tense:

	Present	*Past*	*Future*
Continuous	We are working	We were working	We will be working
Perfect	They have finished	They had finished	They will have finished

(Some grammar books refer to the past continuous tense as the *imperfect*, the present perfect simply as the *perfect*, and the past perfect as the *pluperfect*.) See **shall**, **will**. See also **5** (**a**) below.

3. That which performs the action described in the verb is called the *subject* of the verb:

> *An enormous crowd of passengers* disembarked.

> What train do *you* normally travel on?

To locate the subject, identify the verb and ask 'who or what is performing the action of the verb?'

A verb which has a subject is called a *finite* verb.

4. The *object* of a verb is the word or words upon which the action of the verb takes effect:

> The fire destroyed *most of the street.*

> The library will contain *thirty thousand books.*

To locate the object, identify the verb and ask 'on whom or what is the action of the verb performed?' In the case of the two sentences quoted, who or what is destroyed and who or what is contained?

A verb which has an object is called a *transitive* verb, i.e. the action of the verb is carried over or across (*trans*) to someone or something.

Some verbs, notably the verb *to be* (I am, you are, he/she is, we are, etc.) cannot take an object because they do not describe an action capable of acting upon someone or something. See **7** below.

Sometimes a sentence appears to have two objects:

> The milkman has left us too many eggs.

If one asks 'who or what has been left', the answer is *too many eggs.* This is therefore the object (or *direct object*, as some grammar books call it). The word *us* is short for *for us*, and is called the *indirect* object.

Note the direct objects and the indirect objects (italicised) in

> Please send *me* four tickets.

> I'll give *the dog* a bath.

Here *one* and *the dog* are short for *to me* and *to the dog*.

5. In some of its uses, a verb may not have a subject. Such a verb is called *infinite* (pronounced with the emphasis on the second syllable, *fi* rhyming with *lie*) or *non-finite*. There are three categories of infinite verbs.

(*a*) In the sentence

> To travel abroad costs a good deal.

the verb *to travel* has no subject: the verb is simply stated or named. This form of the verb (usually identifiable by being preceded by *to*) is called the *infinitive*. In the example quoted, we are not told who or what travels; the verb is not limited to any particular subject; the sense is that the cost is high, whoever (an infinite number) travels; hence *infinite*. Note that *To travel abroad* is the subject of the verb *costs* (i.e. it tells us what *costs*).

The infinitive may be in the present tense (*to travel*) or the past tense (*to have travelled*). Infinitives may also be in the continuous tenses: *to be travelling* (present); *to have been travelling* (past). Future infinitives do not exist, but the future can be expressed by using *about to*, as in *to be about to travel*, etc.

It is sometimes thought wrong to put an adverb between *to* and the verb, thus making a split infinitive, as in

> I would like *to fully reimburse* you.

The split infinitive is not wrong, though it can create avoidable clumsiness. It should be used if it feels right or if it avoids ambiguity (Eric Partridge quotes the difference between *to further cement trade relations* and *to cement further trade relations*). Otherwise avoid the split infinitive if it can be avoided without strain:

> I would like to reimburse you fully.

(*b*) In the sentences

> *Driving* along the road, they came upon an upturned lorry.
>
> *Having reached* the summit, we had a splendid view.

the italicised words are verbs without subjects, and are thus non-finite. They are doing the work of adjectives, the first describing *they* and the second describing *we*. Such verbal adjectives are called *participles*. In the examples quoted, *driving* is a present participle and *having reached* a past participle.

Because participles do the work of adjectives, it is essential that they are clearly linked to their appropriate nouns or pronouns. The rule in English is that adjectives or their equivalents must be placed close to the nouns or pronouns they describe in order to avoid confusion. The following are examples of incorrect use:

> Driving along the road, an upturned lorry came into view.
>
> Having reached the summit, the view was splendid.

155

verb

because the adjectival phrases which open both sentences lead the reader to then expect the nouns which are being described. Instead, the sentences continue with nouns which are unrelated to the adjectival phrases. Neither sentence tells us to whom the adjectival phrases refer; they are left in the air, so to speak, without a noun or pronoun to describe.

Similarly,

Being rotten, he threw the fruit away.

is wrong because, grammatically, *being rotten* is linked with the nearest noun or pronoun (here, the pronoun *he*) instead of the intended *fruit*. This can be put right by correctly relating *being rotten* and fruit in one of the following ways:

(i) by placing the appropriate noun immediately after the adjectival phrase, and recasting the rest of the sentence:

Being rotten, the fruit was thrown away.

Wherever an adjectival phrase is used, the noun or pronoun it describes must be placed as near as possible to it to avoid ambiguity.

(ii) by turning the phrase *being rotten* into a clause:

Because the fruit was rotten, he threw it away.

The infinite verb *being* has been changed into the finite verb *was* (a clause being a group of words containing a finite verb, i.e. one with a subject), so *fruit* and *rotten* are now clearly and correctly related.

(iii) by using what is known as an *absolute construction*:

The fruit being rotten, he threw it away.

Here the participle, though infinite, is given a sort of subject, and *fruit* and *rotten* are unambiguously related.

The absolute construction is the equivalent of a clause. *This being so*, we stopped = *Because this was so*, we stopped. The present participle *being* is used idiomatically in place of a finite verb. The absolute construction is a phrase doing the work of a clause. Compare

The orchestra having finished the overture, the lights were dimmed.

The orchestra, *having finished the overture*, went on strike.

In the first sentence, the italicised words are an absolute construction, standing instead of a clause and meaning *When the orchestra had finished the overture*. In the second, the italicised words are an adjectival phrase containing a participle and describing *orchestra*. Note the punctuation. In the first sentence it would have been wrong to write

156

> The orchestra, having finished the overture, the
> lights were dimmed.

because no pause is needed after *orchestra* and the reader would
be confused about the grammar of the sentence. Instead of *the
lights were dimmed*, he would expect a verb of which *The orchestra*
was the subject.

Do not put a comma in an absolute construction.

(c) In

> Swimming is good for the figure.
> I remember coming here previously.
> Paying for the damage does not absolve you from
> blame.

the words *swimming, coming* and *paying* are parts of verbs, i.e.
they are derived from verbs. They have no subjects and are
therefore infinite. They are all doing the work of nouns in that
they are either the subject or object of a verb. *Swimming* is the
subject of *is*; *coming* (*here previously*) is the object of *remember*;
Paying (*for the damage*) is the subject of *does ... absolve*. These
words are therefore verbal nouns, usually called *gerunds*.
Gerunds sometimes are a source of error. In

> The neighbours complained of us holding noisy parties.

what is the object of *complained of*? Who or what is being complained of? The answer is, the holding of noisy parties. The
neighbours did not object to *us* as people but to our anti-social
habits. So the object of *complained of* is the gerund *holding* (*noisy
parties*). That being so, *us* is not the object and should therefore
not be in the accusative (see **pronoun**). It should be in the possessive

> The neighbours complained of *our* holding noisyparties.

as automatically as it would have been if a noun had been used
instead of a verbal noun:

> The neighbours complained of *our anti-social habits.*

By the same argument, note the correct use of the italicised
words in the following:

> I understand *his* (not *him*) being angry.
> There is no chance of the *train's* (not *train*) arriving
> on time.
> The coach told the team that there was every
> chance of *their* (not *them*) winning.

In this last sentence, there is a temptation to write *them* as if it
were the object of the preposition *of*. It is not: the object of *of*
(what was there every chance of?) is the gerund *winning*, and

verb

the possessive *their* is needed just as it would have been if a noun (their *success*) had been used instead of the verbal noun *winning*.

However, there are occasions when clumsiness would be produced by insisting on the use of a possessive before a gerund. In

He resents the French *being called* 'frogs'.

There is no chance of that *happening*.

the object of *resent* is not *the French* but their *being called frogs*; likewise the object of the preposition *of* in the second sentence is *happening*. Thus *being called* is a noun-equivalent, and *the French* should be in the possessive, as one would have written

He resents *their* being called 'frogs'.

Likewise *that*, in the second sentence, should be a possessive, by analogy with

There is no chance of *my* agreeing.

But there is no appropriate possessive for *French* and *that*. This being so, the sentences as quoted would be accepted as correct, and indeed the modern tendency is to drop the possessive form in front of gerunds except with pronouns and singular nouns.

6. In some of its uses, a verb may lack an object. A verb thus used is called an *intransitive* verb (compare *transitive* verb in **4** above):

Waves *rolled* towards the shore.

It is possible for a verb to be intransitive in some contexts and transitive in others:

He *rolled the ball* towards the puppy.

is transitive.

7. Some verbs, of which *to be* and *to become* are the most common, can never take an object and are thus always intransitive.

The outcome *was* as they expected.

He *became* a taxi-driver.

The words following *was* and *became* are called the *complement*.

8. If the subject of a verb is singular, the form of the verb must be singular: if the subject is plural, so must the verb be:

He *is* watching; so *are they*. Do as *he says*, not as *Bill and Ben say*.

To avoid error, think carefully about what the precise subject is:

A pile of clothes were on the floor.

is wrong because the subject is *pile*, which is singular, requiring the singular verb *is*. Errors frequently occur when subject and verb are so well separated by other words or parentheses that when the writer gets to the verb he has forgotten whether its subject was singular or plural. See also **noun 2, number**.

There is must be used with a singular complement: *there are* needs a plural one. *There's only four left* is wrong: the complement is *four*, which is plural. See **there is, there are**.

9. Errors sometimes occur when two verbs are run together, as in

I never have and never shall agree with him.

Here, a verb in the past and a verb in the future are followed by *agree*. The one in the past (*have*), however, needs *agreed* to complete it, though *agree* satisfactorily complete the verb in the future (*shall*). Two statements

I never have agreed with him.

I never shall agree with him.

have been ungrammatically combined. The correct version is

I never have agreed with him, and never shall do so.

It is colloquial to leave the final two words unspoken in such a sentence, but it is slightly clumsy. Eric Partridge goes further and calls such omissions 'bad English; the change of tense necessitates a correct completion of the verb; this would avoid the jolt caused by leaving the auxiliary (here *never shall*) in suspense, like a horse without a cart'.

10. Some verbs ending in -*ing* have come to be regarded as **prepositions**. They include *considering, failing* (as in *Failing that, . . .*) and *regarding*.

Considering his illness, the pressure on his staff must have been very great.

Here, *considering* is not an adjectival participle (of the kind described in **5 (b)** above) wrongly and meaninglessly describing *the pressure*, but a preposition meaning *in view of*.

11. For other information about verbs, see **active and passive, each, either ... or, mood, participle, person, shall and will, subjunctive**.

verbal: concerned with words. To refer to a *verbal message* is usually incorrect because most messages are of necessity verbal, i.e. in words. What is usually meant is *oral message*, i.e. a message sent by word of mouth. Similarly *verbal agreement* or *verbal understanding* should have *oral* if the sense is intended to denote a spoken agreement or understanding. Otherwise use *written*.

Use *verbal* to mean *of words*, not to denote the *method* of communication. It is correct to refer to *verbal confusion* and *verbal misunderstanding* when describing difficulties in understanding words, or to refer to *verbal abuse* when the abuse is in words rather than, say, behaviour.

verbosity is the use of more words than are necessary, and is a fault of style. See, for example, **fact that**.

viable is a biological term meaning *able to live or survive in new circumstances*. It is a fashionable and unnecessary substitute for *feasible*, *workable*, *possible*, etc. There may well be circumstances in which this scientific term can be used metaphorically, but they ought not to include such pretentious verbosity as *more economically viable*, meaning *cheaper* (quoted by Gowers). As always when using metaphor, have respect for the literal origin. And never prefer the fashionable word just for the sake of fashion.

visualise: make visible to the eye; give outward and visible form to (mental image, idea, etc.); call up distinct mental picture of (thing imagined, or formerly seen).

> It is difficult to visualise in the abstract the vast process
> of socialist transformation which is going on in China.

Not so much difficult as impossible, since *visualise* and *in the abstract* denote opposites. The university economist who wrote this sentence presumably meant *comprehend*, *understand*.

vis-à-vis is used only by those who believe, wrongly, that the expression is superior to *in relation to* or simply *towards*, *about*, etc., as in

> The government's policy vis-à-vis the trade unions ...

vowel. The letters a, e, i, o, u are vowels. They are open sounds, the lips and teeth being open when they are pronounced. All other letters of the alphabet are called consonants, requiring the use of lips, teeth or tongue in a variety of closed positions. Note that a consonant may make a vowel-sound in that it may rhyme with one of the five vowels (e.g. the letter *y* in *symbol*). A vowel may sound like a consonant in certain words (e.g. the letter *u* in *queen* is pronounced *w*). See **syllable**, **diphthong**.

vowel-sound. See **vowel**.

W

wake and **waken** have past tenses which are sometimes confused:

Verb	Past tense	Past participle
wake	woke	woken
waken	wakened	wakened

Thus *I was woken (up)*, *I was wakened* (and *I was awaked*, *I was awakened*, but never *I was awoken*). See **awake**.

well 1. Spoken sentences very frequently begin with this word, either out of unconscious habit or to give the speaker time to think. Whatever the reason, the ever-intrusive *well* should be resisted.

2. In adjectival expressions, *well* should be followed by a hyphen: *well-known actor*, *well-kept garden*. But note the difference between this and

> The plants should be kept well watered.
> The team is well trained.

where *well* has the force of a separate adverb, and should not have a hyphen.

what meaning *that which*, *the thing that*, must be followed by a singular noun:

> What we need *is* more motorways.
> What *surprises* me *is* the transport costs.

Here, *what* is a singular pronoun: the writers of these sentences have a singular idea in mind (*What we need* = our need; *What surprises me* = a cause of surprise to me). The singular subject needs the singular verb, and the fact that a plural noun follows should not attract the verb into the plural, as it often does, for example in

> What the town needs are more council houses.

Here *are* should be *is*.

However, if *what* means *those which*, a plural verb should follow:

> The production omitted what *seem* to me to be two of
> the best scenes in the play.

what and which, as interrogative pronouns, are not interchangeable. The former is used in vague contexts, the latter in more precise ones:

> What time is it?
> *but* On which day will you arrive?
> What part of the country do you come from?
> *but* In which newspaper did you see it?

whatever as a pronoun can only be used in subordinate clauses (see **clause 2**, **sentence 4**), as in

> The bank will do whatever is necessary.
> Whatever happens, keep the engine running.

In main clauses, *what ever* is needed:

> What ever can have gone wrong?

See **ever**.

whenever. See **ever**.

wherever. See **ever**.

whether. See **if** and **question whether**.

which 1. As an interrogative pronoun, *which* may be either singular or plural. *Which of the books is to be returned?* means that only one is; *Which of the books are to be returned?* means that two or more are.

See **and which**, **what and which**, **which of the two**.

2. Note the following:

It is a fault which occurs frequently.

The membership fee has gone up again, which is intolerable.

Both of these are correct. In the first, *which* refers to *fault*. In the second, *which* does not refer to any preceding noun but to the whole of the preceding clause: what *is intolerable* is that *the membership fee has gone up again*. In this case, *which* means *and this* (*fact*).

which of the two should be followed by a singular verb, as in

Which of the two versions *is* the more accurate?

while can mean *although*, as in

While his persistence is admirable, it can sometimes lead him into a stubborn refusal to listen to advice.

The principal meaning of *while* is, however, *during the time that*, and unintentional ambiguity may occur:

My wife enjoys the social life of the neighbourhood while I have to be away a lot.

Here *whereas* or *but* would have been more precise. It is to be assumed that *during the time that* is not the intended sense.

while and **whilst**. Both are correct, but the latter is less common than it used to be.

who. The accusative is *whom*, and the possessive *whose*. These pronouns are used of people: *which* is used of things (but see **whose**).

The conjurer who died had swallowed a bullet. (*who* is the subject of *died*)

The conjurer whom the marksman shot at had not rehearsed sufficiently. (*whom* is the object of the preposition *at*)

The conjurer whose trick had misfired was treated by a doctor. (*whose* = of whom the)

whoever has the accusative *whomever*, which should have been used in

Give it to whoever you like.

in accordance with the rule that a preposition (here *to*) is followed by a pronoun in the accusative (Give it to *him*). This is a case, however, where usage (which prefers *whoever* in all cases) is overtaking or has overtaken good grammar. In an indirect question, such as

I should like to see whoever is in charge.

the subject *whoever* is needed, as subject of *is*. See also **whom 1, 2**, and **ever**.

whom is an abused word. It is often used incorrectly; equally often, it is not used when it should be. The rules are not difficult.

1. After a **preposition**, the accusative *whom* (not the nominative *who*) is correct, in accordance with the rule that prepositions are followed by the accusative: *in whom, to whom, by whom, for whom*, etc.

The rule still applies if the preposition and *whom* are separated, as they often are:

Whom (*not* who) is it *for*?

I don't know whom to write *to*.

Whom would you like to speak *to*.

Many people, perhaps most people, would now say *who* in such cases, so much so that *whom* sometimes seems to be in danger of dropping out of the language. For the present, such widespread use of *who* for *whom* should be regarded as acceptable colloquialism but not as correct grammar. Remember *to whom* by the old story of the grammarian who sold his pet owl because it insisted on saying 'to-whit, to-who'.

2. Use *whom* as the object of a verb. Just as one would automatically use the accusative *him*, not the nominative *he*, after the verb in

He's an old friend. I haven't seen him for years!

one should use the accusative *whom* if the same sentences are run together into

He's an old friend whom I haven't seen for years!

because *whom* is the object of *seen*. It is doing the work of *and* (or *but*) ... *him*.

3. Note that *who*, not *whom*, is used in the following, where *who* introduces an indirect question:

There is some dispute *about who was* responsible.

Please let me *know who is coming*.

Here *who* is needed to be the subject of *was* and *is coming*.

4. Difficulties occur when *whom* introduces a clause. Both of the following are correct:

163

(a) He is a plumber *whom* I know to be reliable.

(b) He is a plumber *who* I know is reliable.

If it is not immediately obvious that *whom* is the object of *know* in (a) and that *who* is the subject of *is* in (b), consider the following analysis.

Both (a) and (b) consist of two sentences joined by who(m).

(a) He is a plumber. I know *him* to be reliable.

When these two sentences are joined into one, the accusative *him* has to be replaced by the accusative *whom* (which means *and ... him*). Thus *He is a plumber whom I know ...*

Similarly, if (b) is divided into its two parts, we find

He is a plumber. I know (that) *he* is reliable.

When these two sentences are joined into one, the nominative *he* (subject of *is*) must be replaced by the nominative *who* (which means *and ... he*). Thus

He is a plumber who I know is reliable.

All sentences containing who + clause can be analysed in this way, and it will then become clear whether *who* or *whom* is correct.

The most common error occurs in sentences similar to (b), where two finite verbs follow the *who*. The temptation is to write *whom*, on the assumption that it is the object of the first verb (here *know*), whereas it is the subject of the second (here *is*). The basic construction of (b) is

He is a plumber *who* is reliable

and *I know* is a parenthesis. Think of the parenthesis between commas, or in brackets, and the difficulty disappears

He is a plumber who, I know, is reliable.

If this simple hint had been observed, the following errors (quoted from 'quality' newspapers by a contributor to one of them) would not have occurred:

The bishop was particularly critical of Mr Nkomo, whom he alleged had started a civil war.

The other head in the fridge was that of a beautiful girl whom he suspected was (*i.e. had been*) running with other men.

They and Murdoch, whom it was assumed might be tempted back ..., were the only contenders whom the management considered had enough money.

Monsieur Lovet, whom Professor Maser is convinced is Hitler's son, ... was asked where his father was.

In all these cases the journalists should have used *who*. The accusative *whom* with the verb *to be* in the last example is particularly illiterate (see **verb 4, 7**): one says *Who was your father?*, not *Whom was your father?*

who's is the abbreviation of *who is*, and should not be confused with *whose* (which means *of whom*). See **pronoun 4 (b)**.

whose refers, strictly speaking, to people, but it may be applied to things if it seems less awkward than the *of which* construction:

The colour, whose brightness, richness and purity ...

instead of

The colour, the brightness, richness and purity of which. ...

where the reader may get as far as *which* before realising that he is not reading the lengthy subject of a sentence but a subordinate adjectival clause which began back at the first comma.

will. See **shall, will**.

-wise, tacked on to a noun (*price-wise, value-wise*, etc.), is probably the nastiest thing to have happened to the English language in recent years. It has the advantage of brevity and an air of transatlantic trendiness; it is also ungrammatical, unnecessary and ugly, to be avoided by all but the most insensitive.

wit, in *to wit*, meaning *namely, that is*, is dated if not archaic, and should be used only in legal language, if at all.

with. See **singular 3**.

with a view to is wordy for *to*.

with effect from, as in *His appointment is with effect from September*, is wordy. Say simply *from*.

with regard to is cumbersome for *about*.

woods. Milton wrote (in *Lycidas*)

Tomorrow to fresh woods, and pastures new.

not *fresh fields*.

worth while. In this expression, *while* is a noun meaning *the time taken up*, and *worth* means *deserving*. There are two separate words, therefore, and it is incorrect to run them together into one.

The detour was worth while

means

The detour deserved the time spent on it.

would

The expression should be hyphened when it is used adjectivally (*a worth-while detour*).

would. See **should, would.**

would have, as in *would have liked, would have thought, would have been the first to,* should be followed by a present, not a past, infinitive. It is incorrect to say

He would have preferred to have been there.

One past tense (*would have preferred*) is enough, without putting the infinitive also into the past. Say

He would have preferred to be there.

wrong, though usually an adjective, may be used as an adverb, as in

He added up the figures wrong.

He did wrong.

But idiom demands

The figures are wrongly added up.

Y

you is often used to mean *one,* as in

If you go into a shop where you're kept waiting, you're not likely to go there again.

where *you* means *people in general.* It is ungrammatical to begin a *you* construction and then to shift to some other impersonal construction:

If *you* go into a shop where *one* is kept waiting, *you're* not likely to go there again.

you know and **you see** are very frequently used, quite meaninglessly, in conversation. The habit is often unconscious; alternatively, the words may be intended to give the speaker time to think. Whatever the reason, the habit is best avoided.

yours is never spelt *your's.* See **pronoun 3.**

yourself should not be used as a substitute for *you,* as in

The invitation is for both your wife and yourself.

It should be used only in accordance with the rules set out at **pronoun 4 (e).**

A Concise Dictionary of Correct English

Other dictionaries edited by B. A. Phythian

A Concise Dictionary of English Slang and Colloquialisms
B. A. Phythian

A Concise Dictionary of English Idioms
William Freeman, revised by B. A. Phythian